*Along the Edge of the Tide*

**Also by Kenneth Burnley:**

*Portrait of Wirral* (Robert Hale, 1981)
*The Illustrated Portrait of Wirral* (Robert Hale, 1987)
*Images of Wirral* (with Guy Huntington) (Silver Birch Press, 1991)
*Seasons of Wirral* (with Guy Huntington) (Silver Birch Press, 1994)
*The Wirral Journal* (1982 to 1995)

# Along
# the edge of the
# *Tide*

## Kenneth Burnley

WINTERBOURNE
PRESS

First published in 2004 by Kenneth Burnley at
Winterbourne Press, 12 Leachway, Irby, Wirral, Cheshire, CH61 4XJ.
E-mail: edgeoftide@yahoo.co.uk

ISBN 0-9508289-6-3

Designed and typeset by Kenneth Burnley
Printed and bound in Great Britain

# Contents

## Contents

# Introduction

MANY YEARS AGO, when I was a young adult, I came across a book of essays by A. A. Milne, published in the 1920s. How could I resist picking up a book whose Contents page contained such enticing titles as 'The Unfairness of Things', 'The Happiest Half-hours of Life', 'No Flowers by Request', and 'On Going Dry'?

Having previously read only Milne's *Pooh* books, I was delighted to find so many other facets of the writer's character within the pages of that little book. Most of the essays had already appeared in print in the pages of magazines with titles such as *The Star*, *The Outlook* and *The Sphere*; and, had it not been decided to publish the articles in more permanent form, I doubt whether these little gems would ever have come my way, such is the impermanence of old magazines.

Closer to home, I had previously, through my interest in local history, come across the name of another writer, Dixon Scott, in the pages of the old *Wirral Magazine* of the 1930s. One of his articles, 'Dawn on Bidston Hill', was so full of local colour that I wished I knew more about the man and his writings. How pleased I was, then, to discover a book of Dixon Scott's essays, *A Number of Things*, which contained twenty of his articles, some of which had previously appeared in *The Liverpool Courier* and similar publications. *A Number of Things* contains such gems as 'Ass' (an account of the donkeys on New Brighton beach), 'The Mysterious Road' (a drive to World's End near Llangollen) and 'The Voice of the Storm' (a walk along the north Wirral coast on a stormy winter's day).

But go into any secondhand bookshop, and you will find shelves full of books of collected essays – some of them good, many of them mediocre – but all telling us much about life of the time, for they are usually contemporary writings and give us a wonderful insight into the age in which they were written.

And it is in the same spirit that I present this little collection of my writings to my readers. It is a fairly random selection of articles – mostly new, but some culled from past publications – that, for the most part, are based in and around that part of Cheshire in which I have been privileged to live all my life – the Wirral Peninsula.

However, one of the great things about the place where I live is the sense of belonging to a much wider community. Ever since my childhood days, I have felt a tremendous kinship towards those places just a stone's-throw away: our county city of Chester; the wild and beautiful land of Wales just across the river; the attractions of the Cheshire villages, hills and countryside; and the slightly more distant marcher land towards Shropshire.

Many of the essays were put together on my frequent walks along the beach not far from my home – hence the title – for I have always found the Dee shore a great place for thinking and sorting things out in my life.

So these writings are, for the most part, simply the random thoughts of one ordinary Cheshire man privileged to be living in England at the juncture of the millennia. Some of these reflections will be shared by others: some won't. But whether you agree with the sentiments expressed here or not, I hope you will find the book thought-provoking and entertaining.

For I certainly enjoyed writing it!

*Kenneth Burnley*

# Illustrations

*To those*
*who understand*

# Along the edge of the tide
*Reflections along the shoreline*

I T WAS A SPARKLING early-winter afternoon – one of those rare days between Atlantic storms when the sun shines from a clear blue sky and the horizons are sharp and bright. I'd walked across the hill to West Kirby to post some letters, and, catching a glimpse of the estuary through one of those roads that cut through to the Marine Lake from the shopping area, felt drawn to walk home along the shore. I'm glad that I did. The tide was almost full, but not so full that the sand was covered – all the way from West Kirby to Thurstaston I dodged the rippling waves along a narrow golden strip of beach, in just one or two places having to jump up onto the rocks to avoid getting wet feet!

Westwards, the waters of the estuary rippled and sparkled in the afternoon sunlight, while all along the way flocks of wading-birds – oyster-catcher, knot and dunlin – swooped and swerved, skimming the tops of the waves. Here and there, where the beach remained yet uncovered, lone curlew foraged for morsels among the rocks.

I've always loved walking along the edge of the tide. As a child, and living only a short walk from the Irish Sea coast, we'd often follow the tide out and pick among the shells and seaweed for those gems that were taken home with enthusiasm, only to end up lying neglected and forgotten in some dusty box. Then, as a schoolboy, we'd spend lunch-hours on Egremont shore, skimming pebbles into the inrushing Mersey tide, oblivious of the need to dash back for one o'clock lessons after lunch.

Family times walking at the edge of the tide stand clear in the memory: the fun of toddlers dodging the surf at Hell's Mouth Bay on the magical peninsula of Lleyn, or of searching for crabs in the rock-pools of Anglesey's Church Bay. We've combed for razor-shells at Newborough, and searched for star-fish on Wirral's Red Rocks.

But perhaps the most meaningful times of all have been those occasions when, alone, I've followed the tide-line of my own beloved Dee. It is one of life's experiences that has an effect far beyond its apparent simplicity. Following the tide, with only the lap of the waters and the call of the birds, helps to put life's problems into perspective. One gets a wider view down by the sea: and a smaller view too, for the simple colours, patterns and textures of pebbles, shells and sand offer a fine antidote to the complexities of twenty-first-century living. It's a place for inspiration, and rarely do I return home without the seed of an answer or an idea having been planted in my mind as I've traipsed along the water's edge.

I love the hills and mountains; the towns and villages of my home-land are dear to me; the gentle countryside so full of history, and mystery, I'd not be without. But dearest and most precious of all is the twice-daily lap of the tide on the sands of my favourite shores. As long as I may walk along the edge of the tide, I'll be a contented man.

# Millennial thoughts

*Points to ponder on the last sunset of the old millennium*

ON 31st December 1999, I walked down to the Dee shore to watch the sun go down for the last time in the old millennium. I don't know why I wanted to do it: it was just one of those things that seemed important to me at the time: I suppose it was to do with saying goodbye to the old, and preparing the way for the new.

It was rather a dull afternoon, but there were glimpses of the sun from time to time – just enough to make me want to stay to see it through. If the day had been truly overcast, I'd have most likely given up and gone home to enjoy a glass of wine and some left-over mince pies!

There were surprisingly few who had bothered to come to see the last sunset of the old millennium – a few dog-walkers, and parents with children running through the pools, mostly oblivious to the historical event about to take place before their eyes. It was a good place in which to be on that eve of a new millennium – there was space, and light, and peace. There were lovely views: of the hills, the inrushing tide, the distant sea horizon, the cliffs glowing red, masses of wading-birds – and the course of the Dee up towards our county city of Chester.

And there was time and space to ponder about the past, the present and the future. I went back to the turn of the last millennium, to the year 999: a third of a million sunsets ago. Who, I wondered, was standing on this beach then? A few folk from the nearby settlements, perhaps: people who came down to the Dee not to stroll, or to play, but to keep themselves alive with food from its waters. Looking westward, they would have seen the same hills, the same estuary: greener hills, perhaps, and clearer waters – but they would have little difficulty in recognising the place today. They would not have the incessant roar of planes overhead, that's for sure – lucky folk! – but the clay-cliffs would still be the same, and they'd have the same glimpse of Hilbre that we have today.

So, I thought to myself, we've done rather well to keep this little oasis going these past thousand years – the power stations on the Welsh shore, and the glimpse of industry up towards Shotton excepted.

But, on this final sunset of the old millennium, as the sun sent its last rays across the waters of the Dee, my thoughts turned to the next sunrise, the first sunrise of 2000 – and then again another thousand years hence, to the year 3000. What kind of people will be standing here then, and what kind of a view will they have at the close of the third millennium? Will those far-off hills be clad with the greyness of industry; will the Dee sands be hidden under monstrous concrete bridges; will houses and shops cover our beloved land? The optimist in me said, with more hope than conviction: No, No, No! And, I thought, at the turn of the millennium we owe it to all those who follow us to commit ourselves to keeping the beauty of our home ground intact and complete.

And as I turned eastwards, towards my home, the sky, which had been ash-grey for most of the afternoon, was flooded with a blood-red light – the last light of the old millennium – as if to affirm that my faith, my hope, my assurance, my confidence, were not misplaced.

But only time will tell.

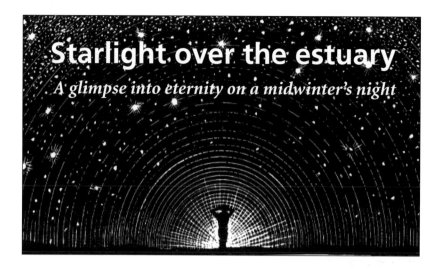

# Starlight over the estuary
## A glimpse into eternity on a midwinter's night

I HAD BEEN TOSSING AND TURNING for hours, unable to get back to sleep. Something close to my heart was disturbing me, and I knew it would be difficult to catch that elusive state when mind and body let go to give me a few hours' respite from my heartache.

I slipped out of bed and, as is my custom, peeped out of the curtains to gauge the weather: a cold, clear, frosty midwinter's night. Beyond the street-lamp, stars twinkled from an inky-black sky, with no moon to diminish their glitz.

I knew then that I wanted to embrace that winter's night in all its glory, all its majesty; and before I realised it, I was striding through the piercing cold of the night towards the estuary. Although my home is on the suburban fringe, with countryside only a stone's-throw away, the street-lamps are still numerous enough to push the night sky into an unseen dimension, but I can escape their pervading glare where the land meets the sea.

Off the road, the frosty-crisp grass crunched beneath my boots as I reached the cliff-top, the darkness embracing me in a friendly, welcoming way – so different from that suffocating darkness we remember from childhood games of hide-and-seek when hiding in that tiny cupboard under the stairs . . .

Standing on that clifftop high above the Dee, I gradually became part of all that was above, below and beyond me: part of the great inky mirror that was the sea at full tide – a black, glassy pool that stretched from Wirral shore to Welsh shore, so still that the stars twinkled in its placid wetness; part of the mysterious night-time landscape that encompassed me; where, on midsummer days I would lie in the long grass, dreaming . . . and part, most wonderfully, of the great dome of eternal mystery that arched high above my head, with the great constellation of Orion in pride of place, striding across the western hills towards the sea.

Lying on the frost-encrusted clifftop bench, my eyes – my mind – felt that same awe, asked the same questions, that our prehistoric ancestors felt on looking skywards in the dead of night. How far? How many? How big? Astronomers and scientists think they know some of the answers, and talk of pulsars and quasars and black holes. They talk of billions and billions – of galaxies, and stars, and planets – and of immense distances to them and between them. But none of them has answered the ultimate questions: How? and Why?

They try, of course, to talk of 'continuous creation', of expansion and contraction, of beginnings and endings. They try to explain it all away in physics, and astrophysics, and cosmological dust.

None of them, though, is brave enough to mention the obvious truth, the reality of creation and existence that answers all my questions on a night such as this: God. He, the source of everything – from the frost-encrusted red-campion flower in the bush where I lie, to the vast cosmos above me. He, too, able to give and take away the very reason for me being here on this coldest of winter nights – that aching in my heart, that *hiraeth*, that longing for something unattainable.

And so I returned to the warmth of my bed, having caught a glimpse that night of something very special: something that I will hold close to my heart for a long, long time.

# An oasis in the High Street

*The pleasures of our secondhand bookshops*

IT HAS NO NEON LIGHTS outside its portals; no fluorescent posters entice the passer-by through the doorway; in fact most shoppers would hardly notice it, so non-descript is its facade. But to me, it is one of the best shops in town. I'll not say which town, for it could be Anytown, as most places have one – and most are of a similar character to that which is nearest and dearest to me. Its wares are well past their sell-by date – in fact that's one of the most endearing features – and you'll not find anything new here. But step inside, and what you will find is an oasis of peace, a sanctuary from the hustle and bustle of twenty-first-century life, an opportunity to browse inestimable treasures with, perhaps, a chance of a rare find to take home . . .

In an age when our High Streets are lined with stereotypical shop-fronts displaying and selling wholly predictable goods, the secondhand bookshop survives because of its individuality – but although each is unique, each having its own special character, every secondhand bookshop that I know has a recognisable 'something' that is difficult to define.

You sense it from the moment you open the shop door – usually with an old-fashioned 'ping' of a spring-loaded bell that warns the proprietor of your approach. Then, that unmistakable scent – for that is indeed what it is – of old books mixed with the faint aroma of coffee. And what a heady combination that is – better even than the smell of freshly baked bread! You enter the shop, reverently, for that is the effect most secondhand bookshops impart – and are struck by the *quietness* of the place. Not a library quietness – that is something different – but the almost holy quietness that you experience when you enter a very old church. Then you notice the emptiness, for there are rarely more than one or two other folk within – and they usually look up and nod, distracted for a moment from their browsings, probably vaguely interested in this newcomer disturbing the peace of the sanctuary.

The proprietor – if indeed he or she is around, for often they are out of sight – will also look up and nod, but (thank goodness) will rarely intrude with 'Can I help you?' Perhaps they know that most book-lovers will prefer to navigate their own way around the shelves – indeed, that is part of the browsing experience. Mind you, I have been in secondhand bookshops where someone flies in, breathless, and goes straight to the proprietor and asks, 'Do you have any books on the rise and fall of the English trout farm in the nineteenth century . . . ?' but such folk do not really belong in these shops: poor things, they miss out on so many missed opportunities to broaden their horizons.

There are two kinds of secondhand bookshop: those which categorise, and those that don't. I'm not really sure which I prefer – it depends on my mood. Sometimes it's delightful to enter a shop where all the books are higgledy-piggledy stacked in unkempt piles, with countryside books rubbing shoulders with astronomy books – for you know not just what you will find next. But sometimes it's very irritating – especially when time is short.

Time of course takes on its own unique dimension once you enter a secondhand bookshop. 'I'll be back in twenty minutes' you say to the wife as you disappear inside while she heads off to Marks and Spencer, promising faithfully to meet her on the dot. But you know what it's like: the proprietor offers you a cup of coffee; you start chatting – about old books, of course – you browse a little more . . . you look at your watch (for I've yet to find a secondhand bookshop with a clock) and you realise your wife has already been waiting 40 minutes.

But what have you found? Anything? That long-lost volume that you've been searching for since 1958? More likely, if you're like me, you'll come out with something you'd never have imagined – something that you never even knew existed. It is unique. It's wonderful. It's a bargain!

But really, more than anything else, the hour or two in that lovely old shop has been an *experience* – for a short moment, you have been in another world and – like you used to do when coming out of the dark cinema after a Saturday afternoon matinee – you blink twice, having forgotten about the big, bright, frantic, noisy world outside. And that's great.

May our wonderful secondhand bookshops be forever thus!

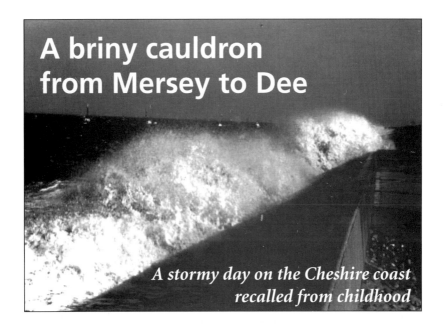

# A briny cauldron from Mersey to Dee

*A stormy day on the Cheshire coast recalled from childhood*

SEASON OF CONTRASTS! Winter brings the colour and warmth of Christmas, and the cold, sharp edge of frosty mornings; the long evenings dozing by the warm fireside, and the stormy gales lashing our coastline; occasional days seemingly borrowed from spring, and those biting-cold, grey days when the wind sweeps down from the Arctic. It is a season in which there is time, on those long evenings, to recall other winters, some distant and others not-so-distant: their pleasures and their joys – their sad times and their bad times.

Childhood recollections of the winter months are few: sunny summer days push out the cold, dark winter memories of our early life. Only the very dramatic, or the very painful, survive. The former are, inevitably, tied in with the elements: I was brought up by the edge of the Irish Sea, and it influenced our lives in so many ways. Dad, brought up in a sea-going Wallasey family, knew of the dreadful magic and power of winter seas. He took me once, in the teeth of a fierce storm tearing in from the north-west, to feel that power for myself at a very early age.

It had been blowing a gale all night, and Sunday morning dawned bright but still very windy: high tide had been about 7am: a 32-footer too! We put on wellies and sou'westers, and trudged along the cinder-track of old Lingham Lane towards the sea. The high hedgerows, though long since stripped of leaves and berries, were a welcome cocoon against the cold wind, and I enjoyed splashing through the deep rain-puddles in my wellies. Within half a mile of the embank-ment, and above the roaring of the wind through the hawthorn hedges, came the thunderous sound of a force I had yet to see and understand. I gripped Dad's hand harder, and kept close to him, a source of security in a wild world of which I was fearful and which I little understood.

We crossed the tramway which served the nearby claypits: the night-time gales had blown the watchman's hut over, and several trucks were lying at crazy angles beside the track. At Lingham Farm, the animals, though secure in their cow-sheds, seemed fearful and agitated at this crazy disruption to their normally peaceful lives. Beyond the farm, we crossed the bridge over the swollen waters of the brook – risen to within an inch or two of the retaining banks – and turned the last bend in the lane onto the Common.

Was this the same green place where, on summer days, I had played with my brothers amongst the long grass and buttercups, chasing dragonflies above the long ponds, and catching sticklebacks in jamjars? For the scene before me, on this wild January morning in 1956, was of a watery wilderness devoid of recognisable features. The high tide of a few hours earlier had thrown millions of gallons of Irish Sea-water over the embankment, flooding acres of grassland: only the tall finger of the lighthouse gave me my bearings.

The track before us disappeared beneath the floodwaters, but Dad knew the way ahead and, carefully picking our way towards the embankment, we climbed the sloping ramp towards the top, the thunderous roar of the sea and the howling of the wind drowning out all other sounds from my young world. Before us was a chaos of white and grey, a confusion of sea, sound, and sky. I was frightened, yet awestruck by this demonstration of divine power in my formerly secure little world. I wanted to stay, to be part of it; yet at the same time I wanted to run away, to be back in our warm little home, with my reading-books and wireless programmes, and all the other things that were part of my familiar Sunday morning. Dad, too, felt this power, this dichotomy of tension between the unknown and the familiar.

We took a last look across the foaming, swirling wilderness, and ran back down the embankment towards the lane and the security of home, passing on the way dead and dying fish swept aground by the waves. On the way home, away from the pervasive noise of the sea, Dad told me of wrecks of the past, and of lives lost, along this stretch of coast. Nearer home, we passed by folks baling water out of their downstairs rooms, victims of the brook that had burst its banks in the early hours of this wild and memorable Sunday morning.

The memory, the details of that early experience, are part of my life still today. When the winter gales and rains lash our window-panes, I relive that day nearly forty years ago when I was baptised into the majesty, the power, the glory of God's creation in this little corner of England.

(This article first appeared in the Winter 1992 issue of the *Wirral Journal*)

# An ancient stone coffin

## *The meaning of life and death in a Wirral country churchyard*

IT WAS ONLY a child's coffin – a casket rough-hewn out of the local red sandstone. But it was old – so very old. Knowledgeable folk said it dated back to perhaps the thirteenth century. I'd never seen one like it, and I've poked around many old churchyards in my time.

I had first encountered it when, as a youngster myself, I had started to enjoy browsing around old churchyards – and that at Thurstaston was (and still is) one of my favourites. The folk at St Bart's had, as with so many churches, gathered the ancient relics in a corner of the churchyard for passers-by to admire. There was an old font there, and probably some old sculptured stones too, rescued from earlier churches on and around the site.

But the coffin was special. It was tiny – no more than three feet long inside – and carved with a specially shaped circular aperture for the head, narrowing at the neck.

Many times, I had stopped and pondered over this relic of bygone days. It's the sort of thing that, especially on those bright, sunny days when the world is great and life is wonderful, and you feel good to be alive, pulls you up in your tracks and starts you pondering about life, and death, and mortality. Even though it is surrounded by hundreds of other gravestones, the starkness of that child's coffin starts you thinking about things greater than your own immediate problems.

The mind goes back to this tiny hamlet 700 years ago, and sees a distraught family grieving over the death of a loved child. It sees a heartbroken father, hammer and chisel in hand, lovingly fashioning a casket for his deceased son or daughter, labouring through the long days to have it finished in time for the funeral. Or perhaps a more well-to-do local family, still heartbroken, has commissioned the coffin from a local mason.

Why did the child die? Accident, or disease? Both were common then; but life was still precious, and every child is special. The child who was placed in that coffin by grieving parents was as unique as the carefully shaped stone casket in which he or she was laid.

Eventually, though, after the passage of time, the child's death was forgotten; as, indeed, were the family, and its succeeding generations: until one day, many hundreds of years later, the old coffin was unearthed during church rebuilding, and carefully laid to rest in a quiet corner of the churchyard as a continual reminder of our own mortality.

Until, that is, that day in the year 2000, when heartless thieves took it away.

No more, alas, will visitors stop and think about life and death in quite the same way as they have in the past.

And that is almost as sad as the death of the child whose coffin it was.

# Buds, birds and blossoms

## *The fleeting beauty of a marcher spring*

EVER SINCE CHRISTMAS, the days have been lengthening. Almost imperceptibly at first: a few evenings of clear skies about the turn of the year, and we suddenly realise that it is no longer gloomy dusk at tea-time, but the western sky still bears a rosy afterglow. The worst of the winter may yet to be, but nothing can stop the gradual lengthening of the days towards spring and summer.

Springtime: a word whose very sound gladdens the soul in the leafless time of the year. Although I write these words in January, my heart leaps at the exciting prospect of nature's rebirth. Yet I see it already, without having to look far – in the bluebell and daffodil shoots, already four inches above the turf – and, no doubt by the time these words are in print, they will be in full flower.

And, as I write, I contemplate the full pleasures of the spring season to be enjoyed in this small corner of England's marcher country. Old haunts rediscovered, and, perhaps, new ones yet to be found. I shall walk the woodland riverbanks of Dibbinsdale on an April morn: one of those fresh, sunny, God-given days when all creation is rejoicing in the wonder of it all. With gold-and-white carpets of wood anemone and celandine at my feet, I shall share with them and the song-birds that freshness of newly born life. The grim and dreary days of winter will seem another world away in those green woodland glades of buds and blossoms.

On other spring days my heart will yearn for the wider, open skies and sands of the estuary. Even here, with no trees to indicate the newness of the season, the sights, sounds and smells of spring will yet be in the air: the very breeze will carry the perfume of newly-formed flowers from the mountains, woods and moorlands of Wales. The wading birds and gulls will soar above the wet sands, screaming with wild delight and exuberance for the warm months ahead. Passing showers will drench me with sweet rain, short-lived episodes of wetness soon dried out by the warming May sunshine.

Sadly, spring passes all too quickly: will there be time enough to experience all the pleasures of this fleeting season? The golden tide of gorse in full bloom across Caldy Hill and Thurstaston Hill; the drifts of bluebells in the woodlands around Raby Mere; the wonder and the richness of the dawn chorus in Eastham Woods; the call of the cuckoo across the greening meadows beside the Dee. The seasons, like a man's life, come, and are gone, all too quickly: the freshness of youth soon grows into the maturity of high summer, and the magic of those early days is soon lost. The flowers will wither and disappear, the birds will cease to sing; the wonders of this precious season – of Life itself – must be grasped and enjoyed while we are able:

> For myself, I only want to live in this green hour, to feel the soft spring rain and see the brave resurrection of life, that life of the fields which knows no death or lasting destruction.
>
> (Richard Jefferies)

(This article first appeared in the Spring 1992 issue of the *Wirral Journal*)

# The yellow and the purple

---

*The magic of the first and last gorse and heather of the year*

T HEY GROW TOGETHER in the same place, shoulder by shoulder; their roots share the same earth, their stems the same air. Yet the flowers of each, bloom at opposite ends of the year. They are the alpha and the omega of the plant world: the one signalling the end of winter, the other the end of summer. And both of them are so much part of the local scene that we tend to take them for granted.

There can be few things in the natural world that uplift the spirit, brighten the soul and give one that 'feel-good' factor than seeing the wave of yellow sweeping across the heaths and commons of Cheshire in the early months of the year as the gorse really gets going. In some years, of course, we have sporadic shows of gorse blossoming right the way through the winter (like the old local saying, 'When the gorse is in flower, then kissing's in fashion') – but even then, the real show happens during March and April, just when we need that tonic to reassure us that spring really is on the way and that winter will soon be just a memory.

And each spring I love to go to my favourite 'gorse places' to see the annual show at its best – on the fine sandstone ridges of Wirral's west coast overlooking the waters of the Dee, or on the foothills of the Clwydians around Tremeirchion and Bodfari, or on Cheshire's sandstone ridge at Peckforton and around Delamere.

Long though the flowering season of the gorse may be, come the hotter days of early summer, and the flowers soon shrivel and fade, leaving only the pods to pop away as the wayfarer passes by on a warm May afternoon.

Then comes a drab spell on our heaths as high summer develops, broken only by splashes of magenta as the bell heather comes into flower; but even as early as mid-July we see signs of the later glory to come, as pockets of common ling show a tinge of mauve – a tinge that will develop into late-summer's most glorious spectacle during August and into September, as a wave of colour covers great swathes of heath and moor in every corner of our land.

This is one of the greatest glories of our north-western counties, a spectacle that never fails to astonish and delight. From Cheshire's westernmost reaches of Caldy Hill in Wirral, right across the county, on ridge and hilltop, to the great swathes of Pennine moorland in the east; and across the great moors of the Welsh highland country – the heather dominates the landscape. Walk through the purple masses on a bright, warm, early-September afternoon, inhale the glorious, sweet scent – this is nature's final fling of the summer. For, unlike the display of gorse earlier in the year, only decay and dying follow the flowering of the heather.

Yet those gorse bushes that so often grow with the heather are even now developing flower-buds ready for the next season. The autumn will come and go; winter will creep along, bringing cold winds and drenching rains to these high heaths, commons and moors. But as surely as day follows night, the tightly-knit buds will slowly respond to the lengthening days of the new year; and, when the sweet, warm breeze sweeps in from the south-west, our heaths will once again blaze with the golden flame of gorse, to gladden the heart and give hope on the greyest of days.

# The old stones by the Dee

*Some thoughts on a spring evening walking along the strand*

IT HAD BEEN a day of springtime showers – the sort that come rolling in slowly from the southwest across the Welsh hills, and still have enough energy and moisture to soak Wirral and to decide for you once and for all that it's not worth going out and getting drenched. And so you stay indoors, catching up on all those jobs that you've been meaning to do – but still frustrated that spring is passing by and you're missing even a day of its magic and richness.

But by evening, the last of the cloud-belts had passed on to drop their rain on Lancashire and the Pennines, and blue sky and sunshine were following. It was obviously going to be a beautiful ending to the day.

It was everything that an April evening should be. Seen from the field-path to the Dungeon wood high above the Dee, the mudflats sparkled and glistened in the evening sunlight. Closer to hand, skylarks trilled high above the pastures, and the woods were full of birdsong. The ground gave off that lovely earthy smell that comes after a day of rain in springtime, and the rains had given the Dungeon waterfall a force that I'd rarely seen, even after winter deluges.

On the Wirral Way, the hawthorns were in full bud, but not quite in flower: that glory was still to come, for a succession of bitter north-easterlies had made this April a cold month. But if these south-westerlies continued, spring would come along in leaps and bounds.

Down on the sands, I trudged past the White Cottage, basking beneath the cliffs in the late-evening sunlight, and found myself on that lonely stretch of beach between the slipway and Caldy. Feeling weary, I sat myself on the limestone boulders that protect the cliffs hereabouts, to watch the sun set. Miles away across the estuary, the Welsh hills glowed softly in the last rays of the sun; but nearer at hand, the reflection off the wet mudflats was intense. And silhouetted against that redness of sky and sand and sun were the heaped blocks of old red sandstone that litter the beach hereabouts.

There was something unearthly about those stones along the beach that evening. They seemed to be on the point of telling me something about their past – on the point of revelation, almost. The sun disappeared into the sea in a burst of glory, the world went very quiet – even the wading-birds seemed to stop their calling – and apart from a rabbit scurrying up the cliff behind me, I felt sure that I was about to be taken back 300 years to see that place as it was when those stones were part of – of what? An old harbour? An anchorage? Ancient sea defences?

But just then, a cold wind swept up the Dee from the sea, and I suddenly did not want to be there any longer, and I strode back along the sands, glad to return to civilisation. Some things are perhaps best left to themselves.

# The greatest loss . . .

*Our society has lost something very precious*

T HIS MORNING, Easter Sunday, driving past a large superstore not far from our home, we were bemused to see many folk turning back from the entrance, puzzled as to why the store was closed. It was a sad sign of the extent to which a Christian consciousness has, during the past 30 years, gradually all but disappeared from the British way of life. These people were prepared to accept the holiday that goes with this great Christian festival, but had no deep-rooted sense of the meaning of the day: it was clearly just not part of their life-knowledge. They saw no reason why the shops should not be open 'as usual' on this most precious day of the year.

Two or three decades ago, even those who professed no acceptance of the Christian faith had an almost instinctual awareness of a way of life that encapsulated much of our inheritance – a sort of 'British cultural Christianity' that extended far beyond the church walls to affect almost every area of our lives: it was a kind of 'manual for living', a social masterplan that, we must admit, made life more pleasant than in today's world where very few have any framework or moral and social codes to live by.

This 'British cultural Christianity' was handed down from generation to generation, not only through families, but also through schools and Sunday schools, government, the media, and almost every organisation that mattered. Very little of it was written down in tablets of stone; there were few rule-books as such: most knew 'the rules' of living, and it took a brave person to overstep those boundaries. Perhaps some of those rules do look a little restrictive today – *but they made the world a nicer place in which to live!*

The great days of the church calendar were, of course recognised with due awe and reverence: everyone knew why we had to keep a solemn air on Good Friday – and I remember that, even in the sixties, we were not allowed to play outside on such days. The meaning of Whitsun was recognised, and most children knew the significance of Lent, Epiphany and Trinity Sunday.

But this culture extended down to our daily rituals too: many families said 'Grace' before starting dinner; and parents would tuck-up their children in bed at night with a prayer or two, after their bedtime story.

Christian morals extended into many parts of communal life, with biblical principles underlying this culture, underpinned by a 'common' belief in God, and of his utmost power to direct and change people's lives. Now, even the very notion of God is reduced to obscenity, with expletives common in conversations and on TV.

That said, almost a hundred years ago folk were despairing at society's loss of religious attention. J. R. Kaighin, in his 1925 book *Bygone Birkenhead* mourned the passing of the faith: 'But what a rebound from the religious life of half a century ago is much of that of today! The line of demarcation between the Church and the world has become faint, almost wiped out. Are we not poorer – immeasurably poorer – for the passing of this "other-worldliness"?' What, I wonder, would he have said of today's disregard for spiritual matters?

And, I too ask: if all that has disappeared from our culture – what have we gained, if anything? And I must answer – nothing! We have actually lost something very precious – something that will be very difficult to ever regain – but are no better off. In fact, it is evident that we are very much worse off. We are a people without a foundation for living. And anything without a foundation inevitably perishes.

The greatest years of this great nation have always been those when our people kept close to their inherited faith; and in an age when we fight to keep the best things from our past, let us not lose that part of our heritage which is more important than rejuvenated buildings or heritage trails: the faith of our forefathers, handed down through the generations for our safekeeping, and sadly all but lost in the past few decades.

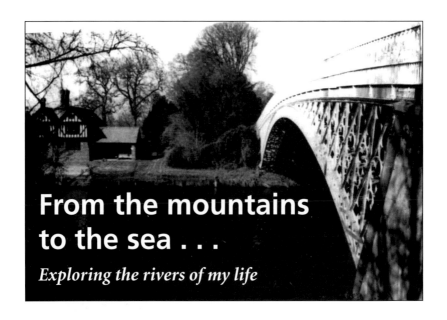

# From the mountains to the sea . . .

*Exploring the rivers of my life*

I SIT ON THE BANKS OF THE DEE at Aldford on a beautiful April morning. Above me, the blue-and-white girders of the Iron Bridge arch majestically over the river. Below, the waters charge hurriedly to the sea, for overnight rains have added to her flow. Behind me, the Eaton woods are alive with birdsong, and I'm sure I catch a glimpse of kingfisher blue darting along with the current.

Dee, Mersey, Clwyd, Conway, Elwy, Ceiriog . . . the names of our local rivers are music to my ears. They are all special friends – all delightful in their own way, but each having its own unique personality, its own character, its own individuality. Some, like the Mersey and Dee, I have known all my life, grown up with, come to know over a long period of time; others I have discovered later in life. But each has figured largely in my life – and rarely does a day go by when I'm not in contact with one of them.

Fortunate to be born and brought up on a peninsula, it is perhaps inevitable that I'd be brought into contact with its boundary rivers at a tender age. One of my earliest photos shows me as a babe sitting on the sands of Egremont shore, spade in hand, the Mersey as a busy backdrop, with ferries, liners and tugboats scurrying about their business. Years later, as a young teenager at school in Wallasey, my schooldays were influenced by the Mersey and its moods: dank, grey, November Mersey mists rising up towards first-floor chemistry labs; the sound of foghorns carried on an easterly breeze; and lunch-hours spent dodging the high-tide waves at Mother Redcap's. The Mersey undoubtedly influenced me more than I realised, for my first published writing was of the river – a short poem printed in my school magazine at the age of twelve or thirteen.

Boyhood days out in North Wales brought me into contact with my peninsula's other bounding river – the Dee. Paddling by the rocks at Llangollen, Mum would tell me to put a message in a bottle, which would be carried down the river and out of the estuary, to be picked up later on the shore near our home on the north Wirral coast.

Then, as a young man, early working days entailed commuting under or over the Mersey to my work in the city. My preference every time was for the ferry trip – wild, winter days when the ferry-boats rocked and rolled their way from Cheshire bank to Lancashire stage, and calm, sunny summer morns when the river was as placid as a lake.

The Dee, though, has been closest to my heart for many years. Most days I walk from my home near its banks to its quiet estuarine reaches; or explore its Cheshire loops between Farndon and Erbistock; or trace its tortuous course through the Welsh uplands. I love this beautiful yet unpredictable river, which has shaped our landscape and our history, whose waters lap the shores of England and Wales, and on whose banks our county city was founded.

Yet our region has other, lesser-known rivers that have played their part in our landscape and our history. The Gowy and the Weaver drain the vast expanses of the Cheshire plain; while over the border, my beloved River Conway flows through some of the most spectacular scenery in North Wales. Between the Conway and the Dee, fine rivers drain the Welsh uplands – the Alun and the Elwy, the Clwyd, the Alwen and the Aled – rivers whose banks are lined with woods and pastures, farms, villages and hamlets.

But on this fine day of early spring, I am content to be on the banks of my own Dee. I sit and watch the dark waters swirling past the willows and the rushes, seeing in my mind's eye the river in its infancy, rising out of the boggy hills above Llyn Tegid, sweeping around the foothills of the Berwyns at Corwen, coursing through the Vale of Llangollen towards the English flatlands of Cheshire, slowing down a little as it enters the meanders at Shocklach; and, after passing this little patch of riverbank here at Aldford, cascading over the weir at Chester, flowing straight as a die through Queensferry, broadening out across the wide sands and mudflats of the estuary between my own homeland of Wirral and Wales, and finally mingling with the briny waters of the Irish Sea beyond Hilbre.

And I suddenly recall some of the words of that verse that I wrote as a boy over forty years ago:

> Sometimes fast, sometimes slow,
> You never know where it may go . . .
> It flows as far as one can see –
> Flowing, flowing, into the sea.

# Walking the extra mile

*Must we lose our traditional units of weight and measure?*

A MONG THE less intrusive features of the Cheshire countryside are those squat triangular cast-iron black-and-white milestones, many of which still remain along the roadsides and verges of our principal highways. Obviously made for a slower era when travellers had the time to stop and read the tiny lettering – Neston 7¹/₂ miles; Chester 17 miles; West Kirby 4 miles – they may become, in time, all that remains to remind us of an age when imperial measurements were the basis of our British way of life; for I've already seen footpath signs in our area giving distances only in kilometres. How long before roadsigns are changed to give road distances in kilometres . . .

We must be crazy to have allowed all this to happen – by 'all this' I mean the gradual, insidious change during the past 30-odd years which has taken away an ancient, established system of daily measurement – of money, length, weight and volume – that was workable, logical and eminently *likeable*, and replaced it with a characterless, modern system based on no logic whatsoever that doesn't even work for most of the everyday things in life.

Take measurement for example. Prior to metrication, we had three very convenient units to use for most things in our lives – the foot, the inch and the yard. All were originally based by the Greeks and Romans (from whom we inherited the units) on sensible, everyday things. The foot, and its smaller partner the inch, is one of the most useful units for everything we use, from picture frames and appliance sizes right through to room dimensions. What is the metric equivalent? Millimetres and centimetres (too tiny) and metres (too large). Have you ever tried measuring a desk in metric?

Go into your supermarket, and you will find your grapes and apples weighed out in kilograms. Now for most things in our everyday lives, the kilogram is too heavy. Have you ever bought a kilo of apples? You get about eight or nine – and who wants that many? So what's the next unit down – a gram: 1,000 times smaller! What use is a gram in our daily lives – useful for weighing mouse droppings, and that's about all! In the old system, we had pounds – very useful for the purchase of most fruit and vegetables – and ounces, another practical amount for everyday use.

What, then, is this metric system that is being forced upon us – mainly by scientists and foreign bureaucrats? It must, one would think, primarily be logical, as it is ultimately to become a worldwide standard for everyone. Logical? It is about as logical as pie in the sky! The original metre was based on 'one ten-millionth part of a meridional quadrant of the earth', i.e. take the distance from the north pole to the equator, and divide it by ten million, and use that as the basis for measuring everything! The new SI metre, however, is even better: it is the distance travelled by light in a vacuum in 1/299,732,458 second! I'll remember that next time I'm trying to measure my next picture-frame in millimetres!

The old names of the past are a feature of our landscape, our countryside. What, I wonder, are they going to do about our English acre – that oh-so-useful area for defining fields, pastures, meadows and other countryside areas? The hectare is commonly used – but that is too big, and anyway it is not recognised by the SI system, as it is non-metric. Perhaps the good old acre will survive, for I suspect that trying to describe land areas in square metres or fractions of square kilometres will prove too much for even the most ardent fan of metrication.

Now I'd be the first to admit that having to learn non-metric units of weight and measure is difficult: remember those long lists on the backs of school exercise-books, and the units of measurement engraved on old wooden school rulers? But the very eccentricity of the names helped the learning process: and, what's more, was the starting-point for an aspect of our country's history and social development. The very names furlong, ounce, stone, had a magic about them. Who can wax lyrical over kilometre and kilogram?

Let's admit it: we've been hoodwinked into accepting into our way of life something alien, inferior, and, to most of us, quite useless. It may be difficult now to turn back the clock: but, at the very least, let us fight to preserve that last, unique imperial measure: the British mile. And those lovely old Cheshire mileposts will not become quaint museum-pieces, but will continue to have a relevance for centuries to come – if only for cyclists, walkers, and others travelling slowly enough to read their message!

# In an old Cheshire churchyard

## *Springtime thoughts about life and death . . .*

IT HAD BEEN a lovely day, Maytime at its best, but regrettably I had been indoors working through the long hours of sunshine. By evening, though, I could resist the call of the countryside no longer, and put the paperwork away for another day. I wanted open spaces, greenness, big skies, trees, and country sounds – an antidote to the words on paper with which I had been working for so many hours – so I strolled down to Thurstaston village, the setting-off point for one of my favourite walks.

Leaving the confines of the village – so peaceful on this lovely late-spring evening – the field-path high above the Dee meadowlands was a tonic. Skylarks – invisible yet insistently present by their continual singing – accompanied me the whole way to Dungeon Woods. Here, where bluebells lined the streamside path, and a cuckoo called incessantly from the leafy depths, was a freshly sprouting, green world, with the evening sunlight spotlighting pools of verdure, and the vague rustlings of birds and small animals in the tangled undergrowth.

Out of the woods, I stretched out on the warm turf of Dungeon Heath: below, the field-patterns of ancient and modern man lay like a jigsaw, blossom-white hedgerows bounding green enclosures with here and there a glint, a sparkle of light on pit and pond. Beyond, the wet sands of the Dee, with their wader-flocks whose calls reached up to these heights, gleamed golden in the sunset; and the peaceful backdrop of Welsh hills and distant skies framed it all, this living landscape picture of beauty . . .

Later – much later, for I must have dozed awhile on those quiet reaches – found me sitting, musing in Thurstaston's ancient church-yard. This, the last resting-place of the country-folk of old, is a hallowed place, with its ancient tower, rough-hewn stone walls, and time-worn headstones. Glancing at the inscriptions, the names, the places, I found myself comparing the lives of the men, women and children of this parish who had lived here in times past, with the lives of today's generation. These people, long since departed, suffered no doubt from many hardships: the struggle for food, for clothing, for a roof over their heads. They toiled long and hard in the fields, in the kitchens, and in their workshops. They experienced illness in all its merciless forms, and many died at tender ages, as the gravestones around me clearly showed.

By comparison, today's generation are well cared-for, with few material needs such as the folk of old knew. Yet I could not help but think that the folk of yesterday led a richer life. They had a simple childhood, free from the pressures that the media impose on today's youngsters. Their pleasures were simple, but pleasures nonetheless. Their world was small, but comparatively safe and secure. They were brought up with a strong sense of tradition in family life, with a belief in the continuity of the community, and were taught a simple but meaningful belief in God and his creation from an early age.

These folk had moral values and traditions with which to grow up, values which stood them in good stead for the trials and tribulations that life flung at them in later years. These same traditions and values, imparted to each generation through the church, the family and the community, gave folk a framework for living, within which they were able to operate. It guided them through youth, through courtship, through marriage and parenthood, through their productive middle years, and into old age. It was woven into the very fabric of society, and the world was, I feel, a better place for it. This important thread has, I fear, been lost today, and although we live in a healthier, wealthier world, we see evidence of the spiritual and moral vacuum at every turn – a generation without a framework for living.

\* \* \*

My evening out, which had started as a simple desire to escape my stuffy room, had taken me on a journey through the spring beauty of a small corner of a lovely peninsula in a small part of this fine land we call England. It had taken me through the mists of time, to considerations of life and death, of human morality, spirituality, and social conditions. And all because I needed a breath of fresh air . . .

(This article first appeared in the *Wirral Journal*, Summer 1995)

# The lone curlew

## *A living link between the mountains and the sea*

A LONE CURLEW flies across a small brook which trickles out of the wet moorlands high in the Welsh mountains. Gathering life and force, the brook leaps down hillsides to become a stately river, tumbling over smooth rocks and flowing gently through quiet, green meadows.

At last, it leaves behind its youth; and flows, as if beckoned by some life-force, towards the sea. Here, with Welsh lands on one bank, and Wirral lands on the other, it broadens out into a fine and elegant estuary, a vast expanse of marsh, mudflats and sandbanks.

The river barely washes Wirral-side, with its old Dee ports and villages, its red cliffs and its sandy beaches. But the Dee still dominates; from our Wirral lands we see the sun set over its wide, wet reaches; we hear its waters racing across the mudflats; and we hear a curlew calling across the sands – the same bird that sped across this river at its birth, high up in those Welsh hills? Perhaps.

(From *Images of Wirral*, with Guy Huntington, 1991)

# No flowers by request

## *A personal view of roadside shrines*

THERE I WAS, happily driving along the Chester High Road on a bright spring day, with not a care in the world, when I glimpsed it out of the corner of my eye: just a splash of colour by the side of the road – a bouquet of flowers, tied to the white-painted railings. I took my foot off the accelerator pedal and slowed down – not much, just a little. My thoughts suddenly changed gear, as the car had done. My carefree mood flew out of the side-window, to be replaced by a focused, thoughtful, definitely sad feeling.

What had happened there recently? Obviously a bad accident, in which someone had died. Friends, relatives, had decided to place flowers at the spot where the victim had encountered death: a road-side shrine in memory of a loved one.

Why? I asked myself.

Initially, I suppose, out of a need to make contact with the occasion of death – a very personal need to try to share in the last living moments of that individual – to share the pain of death, perhaps? The place where a human 'gives up his spirit' is, rightly, a special place – a point of transition, like being born, or being baptised, or married. And many feel, perhaps, that it is right to mark that place in a special way.

But I wonder whether those who set up these shrines – and some do indeed become permanent shrines – realise the effect that they have on those who pass by?

Seeing the bouquet of flowers that morning affected me in many ways. First, it affected my driving. It made me realise that this stretch of country road may contain hazards of which I was unaware, and that I'd be advised to slow down a little, and concentrate more on my driving: just in case.

Then, it made me realise that, in the midst of going about the ordinary round of living, one can meet death. Whoever died at that bend was probably driving to the shops, or taking the dog for a walk, or going to have lunch with a friend – just ordinary, daily things, as I was doing – and never for a moment dreamt that her life would end there, in what is really a very beautiful place. And that gave me much food for thought.

Also, seeing the flowers reminded me of the desperate need we humans have of being able to express our grief at the loss of a loved one. Whoever placed the bouquet there felt a real need to do that – it was an important act, a ritual, a ceremony, with real meaning: part of the grieving process.

And so I continued on my way, but with my day having been turned upside-down.

*     *     *

That was about twelve months ago. I still pass that place regularly, and sometimes there is a fresh bouquet of flowers, sometimes the flowers are dead and withered. The initial impact that the sight had on me is long gone – as I'm sure is the effect on most others who pass by. Besides, more shrines have appeared at other places along this fifteen-mile stretch of country road, each with its own sad story to tell.

My feelings now are that, if it helps, a bouquet of flowers placed at the roadside is a good and natural thing to want to do. But as time wears on, it is perhaps better that the flowers are not replaced; and if a more permanent 'shrine' is desired, that a small flowering tree or a few spring bulbs be placed at or near the spot. In that way, the shrine becomes a healthy, living memorial to a loved one – a memorial that will not wither or die away, but one that will last for ever.

# Sixteen miles to Chester

*A spring
pilgrimage
to our
county city*

O NE SUNDAY RECENTLY, I walked from my home in Irby to Chester: a kind of pilgrimage, I suppose. It was something I'd been wanting to do for many years – follow a trail to our county city – for no particular reason than to say I'd done it. A bit like climbing Everest, or reaching the North Pole: it's there, so why not do it? And besides, it seemed like a sort of adventure – and I'm always game for that!

I travelled light, like all good pilgrims, trusting the coins in my pocket and the occasional corner-shop for my sustenance along the way: if I'd known there were so few of those on my route, I'd have packed provisions sufficient for the sixteen miles!

My way on that fine April morning took me along field-paths and country lanes, through villages and hamlets, past farms and cottages and parish churches – as far away from the main roads as possible. I followed crooked prehistoric trackways, straight Roman ways, Saxon paths, medieval packhorse tracks, a disused railway and, inevitably, modern twentieth-century roads. Each with its own unique character, and each created for a purpose, to lead the traveller from farm to village, from hamlet to parish church, from village to city. And, always, the Dee and its backdrop of hills never far from view to uplift the weary spirit.

I met few folk along the way: the inevitable dog-walker, the occasional fisherman, and just one or two real ramblers. But I did have the joy of spring birdsong all along the way; and the memory of the uplifting song of skylarks high above the Dee meadows between Thurstaston and the Dungeon will live with me for a long time. I also had peace and quiet, and time to think . . .

Footweary and impatient to reach my goal, I was tempted at one point to give up, particularly as the skies lowered and the first spots of rain further dampened the rapidly waning enthusiasm with which I had started my journey. But the pilgrim spirit has always been strong in mankind, and, with the tower of Chester Cathedral now visible on the skyline, there came that primeval spirit of determination to succeed against the odds; and this tired, weary yet fulfilled modern-day pilgrim entered Cheshire's county city as the skies cleared and the sun reappeared.

There were no flags out, no cheering crowds: only the usual Sunday-afternoon shoppers and tourists going about their own business. Unlike the pilgrims of old, in their unique attire, there was nothing to distinguish this Wirral pilgrim from the folk around him. But I *felt* different somehow. I sat in the cathedral grounds with lots of thoughts, lots of emotions. I went inside the hallowed place, just in time to take part in Choral Evensong – the soaring notes of choir-sung Psalms providing a fitting finale to my adventure.

And as I sat in the quiet holiness of that ancient cathedral, I felt a tremendous surge of very positive emotions: of fulfilment, of pride in my heritage, in my ancient county city, and in my beloved peninsula. In those six hours and sixteen miles I had learnt more about my homeland, my fellow-men, and, perhaps more importantly, about myself.

And for those reasons alone, my pilgrimage had been worthwhile. Why not try it yourself some time!

# The cuckoo is not enclosed

*A very special spring morning in Borrowdale*

7 A.M. ON AN EARLY-MAY MORNING, on the slopes of Watendlath Fell. A clear blue sky heralds another fine, anticyclonic day. There are only two people up on this fine Lakeland fell on this rare spring morning – myself and my younger brother, over here from his home in Canada for a few days.

We've left our families still abed in the snug old farmhouse in the village way down in the valley below.

Late last night, under a clear, starlit sky, still showing remnants of daylight at 11pm, we sat, with other members of the family, on the terrace of the village inn, and by the rushing waters of the Derwent, watched a slender crescent moon sink below High Spy as we talked about our boyhood days at home in Cheshire.

Now, we watch the sunlight flooding those same summits with an orange-lemon glow.

When we left the cottage half-an-hour ago, the clean dawn air of the valley stung our lungs with its cold sharpness. Now, warmed by the sun, life is flooding into the creatures of the fells. A pair of buzzards circle the rocks above Great Crag, a family of rabbits nibble the greensward above the larchwoods, and the cuckoo calls across the fells as if his life depends on it.

We sit by the brook talking quietly, pensively, Martin and I, catching up on each other's lives, separated by 4,000 miles, but together now for a brief moment in eternity, 'on one of the most beautiful places on earth' as Martin says.

'But you have the magnificent vastness of North America on your doorstep' I protest.

'Yes,' he replies, 'but here, in these few dozen square miles, is more beauty, more variety, more history, more of almost everything, than is contained in that huge vastness in which I now live.'

And in the quietness of that May sunrise, surrounded by the springtime beauty of that early morning, sitting on a rock with my brother by my side – I feel so proud of England, and all that it means to be English.

We sit a while longer: down below, beside the sparkling tarn where trout are rippling the otherwise placid surface, the tiny hamlet shows signs of life. Farm-hands are hand-feeding a dozen tiny new-born lambs. A tractor coughs into life. England is awakening.

'Right,' I say, 'let's scramble back down to the cottage, and wake the family up with a good old breakfast of bacon-and-eggs!'

And I'm sure I see the glint of a tear in the corner of his eye: or perhaps it's a tear in my own eye.

(The title of this article is taken from Hugh Walpole's novel set in the Borrowdale area of the Lake District, *Rogue Herries*)

# Dusk falls on Moel Arthur
*Magic and mystery on a lonely hill*

Y OU CAN SEE ITS SUMMIT from Wirral's highest places: just one of a chain of domed peaks peeping over the nearer Welsh hills. But this one's special: to me, anyway.

All those Clwydian hills are lovely in their own way: just the right height, just the right shape: fresh green in spring, changing to darker green as the summer wears on, then their brief moment of glory for a couple of weeks in late August and into early September when the heather bursts into flower, and finally turning bronze through autumn and into winter as the bracken dies back.

But these are not just hills (and they'd be wonderful enough if they were): each has its own history – not to tell, but to be sought out. And of them all, surely Moel Arthur is the best.

*   *   *

A May evening, the sun shining from a cloudless sky. I drive up the nant from Hendre, a climbing, narrowing, twisting lane, its hedgebanks a rich tapestry of bluebells, stitchwort and campion, and maytrees just coming into flower – two weeks behind those in the valley, where the blossoms are just finishing. Above the pastures, the hills enclose me as I enter a world of mysteries and secrets.

I park at the Bwlch, the only car, the only person in this Arthurian world of rocks and moors. The silence embraces me: a silence broken only by the cuckoo's call and the raven's cry. On one side, Moel Llys-y-coed, its flank bearing the full evening sunlight; and towering high above me, Moel Arthur, its precipitous slopes in gloom despite the brightness of this fine spring evening.

The path through the heather and bilberries takes me up over the eastern shoulder of Arthur, and I'm glad to be once more in the sunlight as I scramble over the majestic ramparts of this ancient hill-fort. I can see these great entrenchments from my home ground, way across the Dee estuary, and marvel each time at the sheer commitment and courage of those who erected them thousands of years ago.

I reach the summit, and, although I know what to expect, the vastness of the view never fails to take my breath away: and on this clear evening, it is more breathtaking than ever. Low, slanting evening sunshine floods the Vale of Clwyd with light, its patchwork of fields, hedges and woods so sharp in the pure polar-maritime air. Northwards, the sea sparkles in the sun, while turning a little more to the east I see the sands of the Dee estuary and the red cliffs of Wirral catching the sun's rapidly-dying rays. Westwards, the Snowdonian mountains are disappearing into a grey mistiness, the precursor of a rapidly moving weather-front that will bring a day's rain tomorrow.

On such a night, I feel, Arthur would indeed have named this place after himself: and I find a patch of soft turf to lie back on and ponder the great Celtic king and the many legends woven around his life. I'm still alone on this hilltop: but am I? The sun gradually disappears behind the grey mist which rolls rapidly up the vale from the sea, and the air about me suddenly goes cold and damp.

A pair of buzzards flies majestically above the summit: the cuckoo stops calling. I hear stones crunching behind me. I turn, startled and not a little afraid: but it is only a family of rabbits scrambling up the summit cairn.

Suddenly, I feel unwelcome here, a stranger. Turning eastward, I see my home peninsula still bathed in sunlight, and I want to be there. I scramble down the steep slopes to my car on the Bwlch in the gathering dusk, aware more than ever of the power of the past to infiltrate the human psyche, and I drive back down the lane, leaving Moel Arthur and the secrets of the past to itself.

# 'This is 199'

## *A teenager in at the birth of the pirates*

I REMEMBER VIVIDLY the day in 1964 when I heard my first pirate radio station. I was fiddling around with the dial on my transistor radio beside my bed early one morning before getting up to go to school. In those days there were so few stations that one knew them all by heart and their locations on the dial. It was even rarer to hear pop music being played anywhere on a weekday at that time of the morning.

So imagine my surprise when I heard 'Rhythm of the Rain' by the Cascades being played just below the place on the dial where I normally listened to Radio Luxembourg under the bedclothes late into the night! What on earth was a radio station doing, playing pop music, at that point on the dial? Although rushing by then to get dressed and breakfasted for school, I tried desperately to keep tuned to that point – a difficult task, as the sound faded in and out of the airwaves. 'This is Radio Caroline on 199, your all-day music station' came from the announcer. Radio Caroline! But that was in the south of England: how could I be receiving their programmes? 'We are sailing around the coast to anchor off the Isle of Man, where we will be broadcasting to the north-west of England and Wales.'

So started a love affair with Radio Caroline that was brief but ecstatic. Perhaps it was because I was one of the first to hear them as they sailed around to Ramsey Bay – no one else at school had heard them that day – but the pirate station was to become a constant friend and companion for a couple of teenage years in the mid-sixties. From the day I first heard that faint announcement, to the day when they were forced off the air by government legislation, the sound of Caroline was with me all the way.

The music was great – but more than that, the deejays and announcers became almost a part of my life: people – friends – whose voices kept me company in those lonely, still, small hours late at night when the rest of the world was asleep. They became my heroes – and I worshipped them. Other boys perhaps idolised footballers, or film stars: I idolised Caroline's disc-jockeys. Tom Lodge, Tony Jay, Roger Gale, Jerry Leighton, Mike Ahern, Al Turner, Mike Marryat, Don Allen, Ray Teret, Tony Prince. Even now, I hear their names and I hear their theme tunes: and those long, carefree summer days of the mid-sixties come flooding back to mind. I even persuaded Mum and Dad to take us to the Isle of Man for our summer holidays in 1964 so that I could be closer to the source of my pleasure! Seeing the graceful beauty of *MV Caroline* riding the gentle blue waters of Ramsey Bay must surely be one of the most exquisite moments of my youth!

How I wanted to become one of those guys who lived such a daring, romantic life on that ship! School work suffered: I wanted only one thing in life – to become a Caroline DJ. My bedroom became a pirate DJ's studio, complete with turntables and microphone. I pretended to broadcast to the world. I ate, slept and drank Caroline.

Then as suddenly as it all began, it was over. I recall weeping over the closing words of Tony Prince as he broadcast his last show on pirate radio: then the airwaves went silent. The golden days of Caroline were over: oh yes, she would re-emerge from time to time in various forms: but never again would she be the same Caroline that had won my heart in those early days. They say that first love never dies: and, as far as my love of radio was concerned, Caroline was my first love.

Even now, nearly 40 years on, I occasionally play Caroline's shut-down theme, 'Round Midnight' by Jimmy McGriff; and I am a 15-year-old again, switching off his bedside light and going off to sleep with the dreams and thoughts and music of a teenager in 1964 spinning through his head . . . goodnight Caroline.

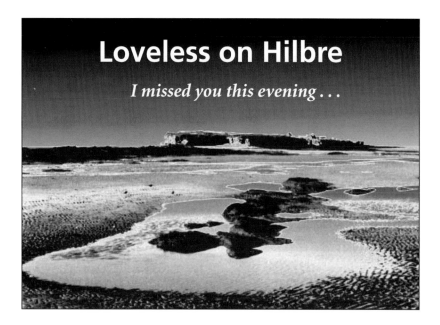

# Loveless on Hilbre

*I missed you this evening . . .*

I LIE BACK ON THE SOFT TURF in the warmth of this May evening, and am intoxicated by the beauty around me. My isle in the sea embraces me as my lover, its arms the carpets of bluebells and thrift, its kisses the warmth of the soft breeze blowing up from the south, its words the endless sounds of waves and birds and breeze.

But on this sensual evening I am alone, and I wish not to be alone. All day I was looking forward to this brief time, hoping you'd be able to come across the sands with me, to share with me beauty that multiplies with its sharing. So many times I've been here on my own, and often I've told you of the wonders of the place. And tonight was going to be special, for you'd hoped to come with me. But for various reasons you are not able to be with me this evening.

All day I've waited for this moment, hoping you'd be able to share it with me. And now, just when I need you most, you're not with me. I close my eyes and dream that you're beside me, that your lips are on mine, that your desire is my desire. I imagine I hear your voice, your words in my ear; but it is only the moaning of the seals on the sandbanks, the cry of the oyster-catcher, the lapping of the restless tide on the rocks; I imagine I taste your lips, but it is only the salt-breeze in the air; I breathe your scent, but it is only the perfume of a myriad wild-flowers around me.

As the sun sinks towards the sea, the sky radiates a million colours; colours that I'd capture for you on canvas if I were an artist. If I were a poet, I'd put in verse the magic that I feel this evening.

When I see you again, I'll try to tell you about all that I've seen, but my words will be inadequate. Perhaps I'll bring you a sea-shell from the shore, and in it you'll hear the waves that I heard splashing on the rocks, smell the brine blowing in from the restless sea . . .

I retrace my steps across the sands of Dee, leaving boot-prints in the silky sand. My loved one, you have missed a beautiful evening . . . but next time I walk across these warm, sun-kissed sands to my isle in the sea, there will be two sets of prints in the sand: mine – and yours.

# 'Bon voyage!'

### *Setting off on an adventure across the waters of Dee!*

I<small>T'S A PLACE</small> I often stroll down to on a summer's evening when I've nothing better to do – the little jetty that juts out into the Dee at Thurstaston. There's usually nobody about by late evening – perhaps a fisherman or two if the tide's right – but it's a grand place from which to watch the sun go down over the estuary. I often stand there and watch the lights come on along the Welsh road across the sandy flats, and listen to the curlews and oyster-catchers calling on the mudflats along the edge of the tide.

On this particular evening – one of those gloomy but mellow summer evenings that follow a warm, sultry day – even as I made my way down the cliff slipway, I could see that there was more activity than usual: not much, but definitely something going on.

When we (my young daughter Helen was with me) reached the jetty, we found a family busily loading a small dinghy with themselves and a huge pile of possessions. The pile would have filled the boat two or three times over, and the dinghy had room for only one passenger at a time, apart from the person on the rudder, who was obviously the father. The tide was rising rapidly, and it was going to be quite a race to ferry family and possessions, in stages, across the quarter-mile or so to where their larger boat was moored, before the rising waters covered the slipway and possessions.

Father gallantly raced family members and belongings back and forth while Helen and I chatted to their Mum, who was watching the proceedings with that sense of concern that only mothers know. One by one her children were taken across to the boat, leaving only herself and a suitcase on the jetty. I'm sure that, even though we were chatting, fears were racing through her mind: 'What if the boat drifts away, with children and possessions aboard, leaving me on this rapidly-flooding jetty? What if Father's dinghy capsizes, or the motor fails? What if . . . ?'

But no, her confidence radiated as we talked. They were from the midlands, and had come all this way with a newly-made boat (made by Father) to try it out for a few days around the Dee and along the North Wales coast.

Father, meanwhile, had capably loaded all the children and luggage onto the main boat, and, just as the incoming tide was swirling about our ankles, had returned to collect Mum. She stepped into the dinghy, Helen and I gave them a final push-off from the jetty, and they sailed off into the darkening gloom of the summer's evening, heading for their boat. We waved them off, and waited anxiously until they were safe on board – a lovely family, reunited again for the start of their expedition.

Helen and I turned around for our walk back home. We'd never imagined that our little jetty by the Dee was a place where people set off for Adventures. And many times that weekend, especially when I was tucked up in the warmth and safety of my bed, I thought of that family out on the High Seas, hoping they were safe – and, above all, enjoying their little adventure around our lovely coastline.

# Crossing the border

*River crossings that stir the soul*

'WELCOME TO WALES' proclaims the sign! I speed past this kindly invitation several times a week, and have done so for many years. But rarely does it fail to send a tingle of adventure down my spine! For a few yards further on, I cross over the Dee, and am indeed in another land – the ancient celtic kingdom of Cymru.

I'm a Cheshire boy and, to most Cheshire folk, Wales is like a second home: my county town of Chester has one foot almost in that country, and barely a day goes by when I don't see her lovely hills and mountains from my home village in Wirral.

But 'crossing the border' still stirs something in me deep inside. Oh, I know that the part of Wales around Queensferry and Flint is not very Welsh, and the landscape here is more English-looking than Welsh. But since childhood days, when my parents would take us across the grand old girder-bridge over the Dee, heading westwards has always verged on the adventurous.

In those days, to get across the old Dee bridge at all was something of an achievement – especially on fine summer Sundays, with seemingly the whole of Cheshire wanting to escape to the green hills of

Wales, and all wanting to squeeze through that narrow bridge. Now, crossing the border is easy: too easy, perhaps, for the sanitised modern road and Dee bridge give no clues of the transition from one kingdom to another: only a quick glance tells us that we're going over the Dee, leaving England behind.

But listen! If you really want to experience the thrill of the border crossing, take the new bridge over the Dee to Flint. I love this new way into Wales – and here's why. First of all, the new road traverses the wide, open expanse of the old sea-lands. Look across the wet meadows to the right, and see the old cliff-line of Wirral; spot the ancient red-sandstone church-towers of Shotwick and Burton peeping through the trees, and the old dykes and gutters of early reclamation schemes along the Dee.

Then, as the new road sweeps westwards, the sun catches the uppermost structure of the new bridge, gleaming white against the hills and sky. The road rises gently towards the bridge – but where to look? Upwards, soaring high above, the wires and frames blend into a majestic, gothic, cathedral-like arch; while below, and to the north, stretch the waters and mudflats of the estuary, with perhaps a glimpse of Flint's ancient grey castle at the river's edge. There are no 'Welcome to Wales' signs here. But, coming back down to riverbank, we truly *know* we are in another land – the landscape tells us so.

This is how border crossings should be: firm reminders that we are moving from one land to another, each place unique and with its own cultures, traditions and heritage. For without that, with boundaries and borders lost, blurred or forgotten, we lose that richness of variety that makes life vibrant and colourful.

Croeso! Welcome to Wales! Welcome to England! Welcome!

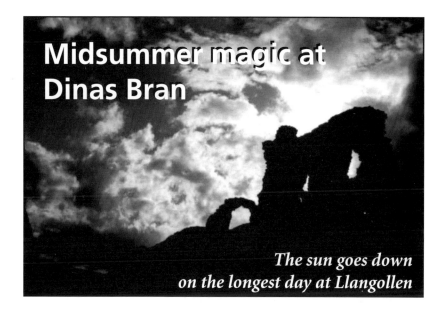

# Midsummer magic at Dinas Bran

*The sun goes down on the longest day at Llangollen*

SUNSHINE FLOODS the Clwydian peaks as I drive southwards for a midsummer's eve rendezvous with the ghosts of the past at Llangollen. June evenings are long, but none longer than this. The names of Welsh villages sing to me as I drive – Treuddyn, Rhydtalog, Llandegla – and the way is bedecked with the midsummer glory of creamy elder and pink dog-rose. But the gentleness of the pastoral marcherlands fades into mountainous moorland as the bulk of Llantysilio Mountain looms large. Crossing the Bwlch is like crossing a frontier – a border between present and past, between light and shadow, between reality and legend. Southwards, thunder-grey skies gather threateningly over the Berwyns, but as I drop down into the Vale of Llangollen along the Horseshoe Pass, the lowering, westerly sun catches the grey-white limestone escarpment of Eglwyseg crags, sparkling against the deep-blue evening sky.

I love this place, this vale of mystery and magic, this place where civilisation meets legend, where forces of light and darkness, of Christianity and paganism have battled over the centuries among the cwms and crags. Since boyhood I have explored its paths and tracks, its holy places, its wells and springs, have followed in the footsteps of princes and warriors, have traced the flight of monks and abbots. On soft November afternoons I have sat on the crags at World's End, and seen the mists rise up the valley as dusk falls; on sparkling April morns I have followed the lively, feminine Dee as it tumbles over rocks and through ravines, its waters icy-cold with spring snow-melt from distant hills. On frosty January morns I have stood within the hallowed, broken walls of Valle Crucis and watched the sun rise over the Ceiriog hills. And always, a sense of wonder, of mystery and magic.

But my eyes, my heart, my feet always turn to Dinas Bran, the castle on the hill. Sometimes I drive along the vale from Pontcysyllte, from which direction the castle always looks majestic, lordly, high above all. Coming down from the Horseshoe Pass, as I am this evening, the castle looks tiny, insignificant, overshadowed by the higher hills and crags around. The best, though, is the approach from World's End, when Dinas Bran suddenly bursts into view as the lane turns east towards the town.

Why am I here on this midsummer's eve? I know not: something deep inside just brought me here. A special place for a special occasion? Indeed – and this place is very special. Here we have connections with the Britain of Arthur and the Holy Grail; of the unrequited love of one of Wales' greatest poets for Mevanwy Vechan, the fairest of maidens, who lived in the castle; below these walls fled the monks of Bangor-on-Dee from the butchery of Aethelfrith to a new life beyond the hills.

But on this bright, blustery, showery June evening, as I scramble up the steep path to the summit, things other than legends fill my heart: for here is a veritable wild garden of colour, from the majestic fox-gloves in the lush lower meadows to the smaller but no less beautiful plants that cover the thinner, stony turf around the ramparts: eye-bright, bedstraw, and the pink and yellow star-flowers of stonecrop. On the ruined walls, small ferns and purple bellflowers cascade to the floor. Later in the summer, harebells and meadowsweet will blossom on the lower slopes.

And so I sit, alone, on the topmost stones of Dinas Bran on this midsummer evening, the year 2000. To the west, the sun still shines from a sky bedecked with white cottonwool clouds. Coming from the south, the thunderclouds I had seen earlier are drawing closer, putting the town of Llangollen into shadow. I take shelter in the lee of the broken walls, but the main storm passes to the east, where a double-rainbow crosses the vale from Eglwyseg to Ceiriog. Both rain and rainbow are soon gone, and once again the sky becomes blue; then, as the sun lowers, turns to silver, then gold. The stones around me glow in the evening light, as they have done for a thousand years or more. All about me, comes the whisper of indistinguishable sounds – tales of long ago, or simply the wind blowing through the gaps? Who knows?

But I will not see the sun go down over Llantysilio Mountain tonight, for another storm looms up from the west, filling the air with a gloom that, perhaps, befits this late hour. Dinas Bran has its secrets – secrets that I had hoped to discover on this special eve – but it is not prepared to share them with anyone, not even on midsummer's night.

And so I make my way down to the lane to the car; but, as I cross the green meadows below Eglwyseg, I am sure I hear the cry of a maiden from the lofty, rocky heights of Bran: or perhaps it is the call of a bird flying above the ruins: a crow, perhaps; for that is the meaning of Bran in Welsh.

And I give a slight shudder in the growing coldness of the night air and, on this shortest of nights, leave Dinas Bran to its secrets . . .

# Black Harry's

## *A mysterious place not far from home*

For years, my dad had talked about Black Harry's: to me, a preteen child in the 1950s, it fell into the same category as Heaven, or Hell: one of those places that adults talked about, and assumed that we understood too, but never really explained what they really were.

Gradually, I came to realise it was just over the electric railway line from our house: from our window we would see folk walking by the fence: 'Going to Black Harry's', Dad would say. I never thought – dared – ask, 'What for?'

Then, one hot, summer's day, after school, Mum said, 'We're going to Black Harry's'. I still didn't know whether to be overjoyed or dismayed. What if it turned out to be something terrible, like a visit to the dentist, or worse . . . but Mum was packing a picnic as she spoke, so I knew it couldn't be anything like *that*.

'Find some string, and some hooks: we'll use an old stick for a rod.' And then it dawned – we were going *fishing*.

A twenty-minute trek across buttercup-filled meadows brought us to that path by the fence on the other side of the railway that I'd only ever seen from home. Now we were on it, and I could see our house! And Black Harry's was all that a mysterious place should be: a dark pond, bordered by dense bushes and grassy banks. Mum found a patch of greensward, and while she sat in the late-afternoon sun, we (for my two younger brothers were with us) played hide-and-seek in the bushes, caught a couple of sticklebacks, and waved to the homeward-bound commuters on the trains.

Later – much later, as the afternoon warmth turned to evening coolness – older boys came to the pond, with girls at their side: but they did not fish, or play hide and seek . . . they just seemed to disappear. We thought nothing of it – but Mum knew then that it was time to head home . . .

That was the first of many happy trips to Black Harry's. A few years later, Mum let us go there on our own – as long as we crossed the line by the crossing. We knew, though, of boys who crossed the line where the live rails ran knee-high above the track. We admired these daredevils – until one dreadful day, when we heard that one had tripped, and been electrocuted to death on the live rail.

Years later again, we returned to Black Harry's on summer evenings: not with mates, or brothers, but with a girl by our side – and we knew then what those older boys and girls had got up to as Mum had dragged us home. And even now, the scent of May blossom and wild roses, the flash of dragonfly wings across still waters, evoke images of first-fumblings of youthful desire and the loss of childhood innocence.

As children, we returned home from Black Harry's with Mum, tired and happy with a jamjar full of sticklebacks and tadpoles; as youths, we traipsed home arm in arm in the summertime dusk, hair tousled, clothes dishevelled, hearts beating fast with the joy of first romance.

* * *

I've never gone back to Black Harry's: never wanted to return, to find that it's either been filled in, or smartened up. I'd rather remember it the way I've always remembered it: a magical, mysterious place of hot summer days: a place where children became boys and girls, where boys became men, and girls became women. And a place where summer was for ever.

## Our secret places

WE ALL NEED THEM: those places where we can go when the need arises. I call them my secret places, for most of them are very remote, out-of-the-way places which few folk know about, and which are therefore almost always very quiet, and peaceful. I'm not going to name any of my special places, but some of you may be able to guess their location from my descriptions.

It has always been important to me to have these places in my life. I can still recall my very first 'secret place' that I discovered when I was about eight or nine: it was just behind the house where we lived: a wild, grassy corner where, in summer, buttercups and lush, long grasses flowered in profusion. I think I first discovered it while playing hide-and-seek – it must have been very secret, for no one could ever find me there, and yet it was only a stone's-throw from 'block'. I'd often sit there, alone, on warm summer days, just listening to the sounds of the neighbourhood, perhaps fiddling with the grass-stems and flowers. Sometimes I'd forget I was playing hide-and-seek, such was the wonderful sense of isolation I felt in that secure place. No one else ever knew about it – and that's what made it special – and secret.

Even later, as a teenager, I had these places. One was beneath some thorn bushes alongside some old marl-pits on the meadows near our home. Here, away from the family and friends, I had time and space to sort out for myself all those problems that beset young men venturing out into Life and the World. There were always birds, and insects, and fish jumping out of the water: always something to watch, to take my mind away from whatever was disturbing me. And, after a half-hour in the cool shade of the bush, I'd emerge, perhaps no happier, but with something like a fresh perspective on the situation.

Now, I have many secret places to which I can take myself: always somewhere to suit my mood, my frame of mind. Some of these places are ancient buildings where the life-forces of centuries have given the place some special power to heal and energise. Many are churchyards, where the magical blend of nature and religion and eternity combine to give the place a special meaning. Some are mountains, where the forces of weather and geology overpower all else, but where the heart can lift itself to the sky. Many are by the sea, for there is nothing like the combination of sea, sky and wind to clear minds weighed down by the cares of the day. But most are just bits of local countryside where, for some reason, everything comes together in a special way: a quiet piece of woodland, perhaps, or a rocky estuarine outcrop, or a wooded dingle by a stream, or a meadow where some particularly lovely flowers grow.

I need these special places in my life, for lots of reasons. I need them when I am happy, and when I am sad: I need them when I'm full of energy, or feeling low; and, understandably, I get quite angry when something intrudes into any of my special places, to change them or destroy them, for they are like the rooms in my house, to be jealously protected and guarded against those who would interfere.

Do you have any secret places in your life?

# Too busy on a Sunday

## *The sad decline of the 'specialness' of our Sundays*

WE HAVE ALWAYS ENJOYED a day out in Chester. As children we would often be taken on a Saturday into the city centre to do some 'special shopping' for new school-clothes or, nearer Christmas, to do our Christmas shopping. I loved those days: the hustle and bustle of the shoppers, the traffic, the buzz of life that permeated the city.

Sometimes, too, we would go into Chester on a Sunday afternoon: but that was quite different from the Saturday experience. There was hardly any traffic in the city, and we'd park quite easily down by the Groves. We'd walk along by the Dee, then along part of the Walls, through the main shopping-streets which were quite deserted – only leisurely window-shoppers like ourselves out and about in the after-noon sunshine. Above all was an all-pervasive sense of peace and quietness. It made one feel good – relaxed, at ease with life. After watching the swans and ducks down by the river, and perhaps enjoy-ing an ice-cream cornet, we'd drive leisurely back along the Chester High Road, in time for a typical Sunday afternoon tea of ham-salad and home-made coffee cake. And during the evening we'd realise that the new week was about to begin as Mum prepared us for school and the days ahead. But the oasis of Sunday – the special day – had been a perfect buffer between the stresses and duties of the old week and the coming cycle of the new.

Now, we've lost that special day of the week. It has gone for ever, lost to the dreaded god of secular materialism. Go into Chester now on a Sunday afternoon, and it seems no different from any other day of the week. The peace, the magic, the sanctity have gone. Something that was extremely valuable to the human condition – something that made our lives richer – has been sacrificed on the altar of greed and commerce, and we have let it happen with barely a murmur of complaint.

Of course, many do not know what they have lost – for they have grown up in a seven-days-a-week whirl of dash-and-grab, not knowing that there was, until quite recently, one day in seven when, from the moment of waking up, we knew – could sense – that it was Sunday. There was something in the air – a quietness – that told us it was special. There was less traffic about – for the only places open on Sundays were churches and newsagents. People lived and behaved more quietly too, for there was a social awareness that this was a 'holy' day, and there were certain things that one avoided – such as letting children play noisily outside, or rowdy 'do-it-yourself' jobs.

Today, sadly, a generation has grown up not knowing of the uniqueness of Sundays. It is a generation that thought it could make itself happier by throwing away all those traditions and values which were seen as 'old-fashioned', but which is now wallowing, thrashing around, with no sense of direction. There was a lot of sense in keeping Sundays special – common sense, really: a body, and its soul, needs a regular time of refreshment. It needs breathing-space away from noise, and rush, and commerce. It needs time to stop, to think, to just occasionally do nothing.

Many, sadly, thought that those who wanted to change Sunday could do so, while the ones who wanted to keep it special, could do so too. Freedom of choice, it was called. It didn't work though: for the activities, the noise of those who want to keep busy on Sundays intrudes on those who want to keep it special. So we all suffer.

But we can change. If we stop shopping on Sundays, the supermarkets and shops will not consider it worthwhile to remain open. Instead of dashing around in our cars, we can take a local walk, and in so doing, perhaps discover the smaller, quieter beauties around us – in the plants, and birds, and butterflies.

Who knows – one day, perhaps, we will again be able to walk around our towns and cities on a Sunday afternoon and enjoy the peace, the quietness, the sheer tranquillity of what is still – to me and to many – the special day of the week.

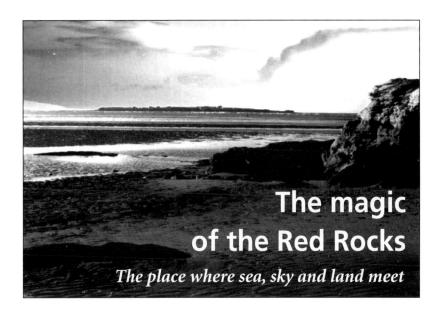

## The magic
## of the Red Rocks
*The place where sea, sky and land meet*

THE TIP OF WIRRAL, it is often called – the journey's end. From Chester, and along the High Road, the signs all point to Hoylake. From here, the road goes no further. Next stop: Ireland, across the restless Irish Sea. In the old days, when sailing-boats carried passengers from Wirral to Ireland, this was the last sight they had of Cheshire-land, this bright, wind-swept, rocky tip of Wirral.

This is river's-end too. This is where that great river, the Dee, after its long and often tortuous journey from Welsh highlands, through Cheshire lowlands, loses its identity and becomes one with the sea, a river no more.

This is a wonderful place, this wild land's-end of Cheshire. I have known this place in all seasons, in all weathers, at all times of day and night. On golden summer afternoons when the dunes are bedecked with their colourful display of wild flowers, and butterflies dance from plant to plant.

I have seen this exposed corner of Wirral ravaged by January gales sweeping in from the Irish Sea, the estuary a boiling grey cauldron of foam and spray. And I have walked along the beach on cold, clear, frosty January nights, the heavens a vault of blackness above the estuary, the stars of Orion dominating all, and the lights of buoys and light-vessels scarcely a glimmer across the endless, inky expanse of sea.

Jutting out into the estuary are the Red Stones, in ancient times the limit of the jurisdiction of the port of Chester. Stand on these rocks on a fine, clear summer's day, when the breeze blows in from the west, and take in the sky, the sea, the air – air which is probably among the purest in England, having traversed miles of sea, moorland and mountain. Look southwards down the Dee, along the Wirral coast-line. Westwards, towards the estuary, with the Hilbre Isles and, beyond, the hills of Wales. In the far distance, the Ormes of Llandudno, and perhaps a glimpse of Anglesey. Northwards, to the sea horizon, and occasionally the faint silhouette of Cumbrian and Scottish hills.* And eastwards, along the north Wirral coast, to Lancashire and the Mersey, to lands of commerce and industry.

But these are all far away. Red Rocks itself has more than enough to offer, in its flowers, its birds, and its wildlife: beauty to complement the scenic backdrop beyond.

(This piece originally appeared in *Seasons of Wirral*, 1994)

---

* Since this piece was published, a cluster of wind turbines has been placed out beyond the estuary, spoiling for ever the unique sense of place that used to be the very special attraction of Wirral's Red Rocks.

# A sense of identity

*Some thoughts about who we are . . .*

'THE NORTH' declares the motorway sign as I leave London and start the long drive home after a business trip to the capital. A week or two later, after a couple of days in the Lakes, I head towards the M6 from Windermere. 'The South' declares the motorway sign as, once again, I drive home. So, am I a Northerner, or a Southerner? That, of course, varies according to the perception of who is asking the question. To a Londoner, I am, almost without question, a Northerner. But perhaps, to a real Northcountryman, a Dalesman or Cumbrian, I am indeed a Southerner.

However, I don't regard myself as either, for both terms carry stereotypical images which, I'm sure, do not fit me! At least, I do not perceive myself as either of those!

Perhaps I'm a Midlander, for the part of England in which I live is, geographically speaking, in the middle belt of England. But surely the Midlands is that area in and around Birmingham – and that is as remote in every way from Cheshire as York is from Cornwall. No, don't call me a Midlander, for that tag implies a sort of grey, nowhereness, nondescript kind of location. And I'd really hate that!

My part of the world is usually classified, by weather forecasters, train operators and the like, as the North-West. I like that. It's got a feel of being somewhere a bit different, of being slightly out on a limb, akin to the Northwest frontier of India, or the wildernesses of

Alaska. It has a youthful zest to it, for in the title there are links to the cool, fresh, straight-off-the-sea winds that often blow in across these parts from the north-west. Yes, I can live with that.

But we're only on the edge of the North-West: the lower, left-hand corner, if you like. Again the true North-West is Lancashire and the Lakes. And what about North Midlands? No, that's more like the Stoke/Derby area, landlocked, not really us.

What about Welsh border country – now that's more like it! This bit of England is only just England, and its history is so closely tied in with that of Wales that it is indeed right to call it 'border country'. But to call myself a 'Welsh border countryman' is something of a mouthful, so I'll have to think again.

Perhaps, though, the problem is really to do with trying to categorise folk by their place of residence. It stems, to some degree, from a Londoncentric attitude that has persisted in this land for centuries, and which has resulted in a bias in culture, attitudes and perceptions that will take further centuries to erase.

I am a unique blend of genes, here today in this part of Great Britain as the result of thousands of years of intermingling of cultures. I am an Englishman with Welsh, Yorkshire and Westcountry blood, living in Cheshire county in the north-west of England on the Welsh border, from where I can, on a clear day, see the kingdoms of Wales, Scotland and Man, and within a ferry-trip of Ireland. All of those places have affected, and continue to affect me and are part of my heritage.

And I am truly proud of this melting-pot of cultures that has made me 'Me'.

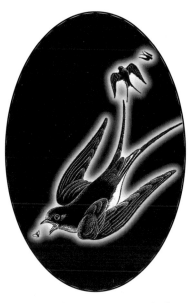

# The last swallows of summer

## An enchanting September afternoon in the Clwydians

THEY TOOK ME by surprise – utterly! I came to this remote place on this bright, late-September afternoon because I was feeling a bit sorry for myself. It's an ancient hillfort – one of many that crown the high ridges above the Vale of Clwyd – on a westerly spur of Moel Fammau: an uplifting, breezy place that always catches the sun, even when the summit of the mountain is cast in cloud, like it is today.

Scrambling down through the knee-deep bilberry, heather and gorse – patches of which are still showing remnants of summer colour – I was aware that there had been few birds on the moors on this lovely afternoon, despite the warmth and the sunshine. But as I came down to a little cwm just below the Moel, there they were – fifty or sixty swallows, darting, diving and gliding in and out of the clumps of gorse and bracken, never more than a foot or two above the turf.

And, more than the fresh, soft, invigorating breeze that's blowing across the vale from the mountainous west; more than the warm sensuality of the September sun on my face; more than the breathtaking panorama of sky and sea and cloud and hill; and more, more than any and all of these things, the sudden sight of those swallows has lifted me up above – way up above – all those stupid little things that were bothering me. And that's strange, for really I should perhaps be feeling slightly sad that summer's nearly over and the birds are

67

gathering to start their autumn migration. But seeing these beautiful creatures so gracefully swooping above the hillside, so enjoying the warm air, the freedom, the very joy of existence, humbles me, takes me above my earthly cares to where they are: enjoying the freedom of the sky, the air, the breeze . . .

They remind me too of the joys of the summer just gone, and of summers past: of places home and away in which the swallows have accompanied me on my jaunts: of the excitement of seeing the first swallows of spring, flitting about the churchyard at Eccleston by the Dee; of the pair that accompanied our late-night hike along Borrowdale one achingly beautiful summer's evening in the Lake District; of the lone swallow that skimmed the lakelike waters of the Dee estuary one June evening as I walked wearily back to the shore; and of the many small flocks that return year after year to our local villages, hamlets and farmyards.

I sit on the warm turf of the entrenchments looking southwards towards the ranges of hills and mountains beyond the vale – Llantysilio Mountain, the Berwyns and beyond. Soon these delicate birds, flying now high above me, will have a long, long journey to face – a journey that begins here, but will take them thousands of miles across land, sea and desert, through wind and storms, against the hazards of both man and nature.

Today, though, they are living life to the full. I can almost hear their shrills of delight as they interweave with each other, using the updraughts to take them soaring higher and ever higher, then gliding earthwards to scoop up moths and other insects from amongst the heather and gorse bushes. They are enjoying life while they can, without fear of tomorrow.

And I take up their message with my rucksack. Almost running down the hillside, I take one last look back to the ancient mound which, perhaps, the ancestral families of these swallows visited in prehistoric times, and feel a better man for my experience of seeing the last swallows of summer . . .

# Nuts, muttons and quads

### *Craftsmanship in an old Wallasey air-raid shelter*

IT WASN'T A VERY glamorous place really: just a brick-and-concrete air-raid shelter tucked away in a forgotten corner of the school playing field. From the outside it looked nothing; but to step inside was to enter another world – a world where folk spoke a strange language, where the air was thick with the smell of ink and paraffin, and in which the visitor felt to be an intruder in some secret clan.

Step inside at 4.30pm on any weekday and, once past the rakes and mowers and other paraphernalia belonging to the school groundsman, you would normally have seen four or five young boys in smart school uniform earnestly busy with their hands – and, indeed, from the expressions on their faces – their brains too. Along one side-wall would have been a lad or two standing before green trays containing dozens of small compartments, from which they would be assembling small pieces of shiny, silvery metal. Another boy would be pulling smaller green trays from a vast array of similar trays on the opposite wall – trays labelled with such strange-sounding names as 72 Perp. Tit., 48 Gill Bold Cond., and 24 Leaders and Emeralds. Away in the far corner of the air-raid shelter an older boy would be treadling away at a primitive-looking but impressive and very noisy contraption into which he carefully placed sheets of paper or card, retrieving same at a rhythmical pace on completion of the cycle.

Mostly, apart from the clackety-clack rhythm of the machine, the room was quiet; but occasionally one of the boys would pipe up: 'John, could you pass me some 6-point leads' or 'Paul, have you seen the mallet and planer?'

This was Wallasey Grammar School Press in the 1960s.

Many schools had their own printing presses in those days, usually set up by enterprising masters to cater for the publicity needs of rugby teams, after-school societies and the like. Today, of course, word-processors and desktop publishing setups serve the purpose; but the old school presses were real printing houses, in miniature – and Wallasey's was one of the best. Run for most of its days by much-loved Physics teacher Jack Dugdale – the Master of the Press – competition was keen among the many boys who wanted a coveted place in the Press. I waited an interminably long year and a half before being invited to join, and I still recall the ache in my heart every time I saw the words 'Printed at the Wallasey Grammar School Press' on the back page of a concert programme, with the ancient emblem of a medieval printer pulling the handle of an old wood-press. How I wanted to be part of that secret and mysterious band who went down to the air-raid shelter in the corner of the playing field every evening . . .

Then, one spring day after school, the Master came up to me and asked me to put out my hands for inspection. 'You'll make a good compositor' he said after checking my hands carefully. 'Would you still like to join the School Press?' To this day I do not know what he was looking for: perhaps long, dextrous, nimble fingers that could dart amongst the countless tiny pieces of metal type; perhaps finger-nails that were not too well manicured or too clean (but then what 14-year-old boy's nails are?). Little did I know then that my enthusiastic response to join was to be the start of a lifetime in the business of putting words on paper in one form or another and a love of letter-forms in all their guises . . .

Entering that den of activity for the first time was indeed an initiation into something that I found exciting beyond my wildest dreams. But it was intimidating too – everyone seemed to know exactly what to do: how would I ever get to know the countless typefaces, the strange tools of the trade and, above all, the mysterious language that they talked? But learn it I did, and soon my name appeared at the bottom of the prominent board that hung on the brick wall listing the Members of the Press: from Master of the Press at the head, down through Senior Journeymen, Journeymen, Apprentices, to lowly Novices, of which I was the lowliest.

From the moment I entered the old shelter on that spring evening, I knew that I wanted to be involved in the printed word as my lifetime's career: I was drawn in to the magic of putting letters into words, words into lines, and lines into pages. I succumbed to the thrill of deciding which typeface to use from a thousand, whether to place a full stop before or after a quotation mark, and whether to use bold or italic for a headline. The smell of printing ink was like a drug: I would wait eagerly by the printing press to see the first impression of my careful compositing, then take it away to check, hoping that there would be few, if any, errors. Then, pride would fill my heart when I saw the finished 500, or 1,000 copies, distributed throughout the school.

In those moments I felt the power of the printed word to mould, to change, to influence people's lives – and I wanted to be a part of that. In those early years I knew that I wanted to be a communicator: and nearly 40 years on, I am delighted to be still communicating through the printed word.

And to think it all started in a tiny air-raid shelter in Wallasey . . .

(PS: nuts, muttons and quads? They are all printers' terms for spacing units used in setting type)

# The spirit
# of the hills

---

*A beautiful September after-noon on a Clwydian hilltop*

Y‎ou can see it from some of Wirral's higher places, but it looks nothing spectacular – just a small hilltop showing above the nearer line of hills that border the Dee estuary. But when the early September sun catches its summit on one of those clear, bright afternoons that we often get in late summer, you catch a teasing glimpse – a pale purple haze – of the beauty that entices me to its bosom time after time.

To some, hills are there to look at – a part of the landscape that, perhaps, flits by as the car travels on to somewhere else. Others see them as objects to be conquered, hiked over as quickly as possible – get to the top, admire the view, sprint down to the valley again.

Hills, to me, are like a glass of good wine: the excitement lies in the anticipation of pleasures to come; in the long-drawn-out savouring of their delights; and in the lingering afterglow and memories of a beautiful experience . . .

And so I find myself on this lovely September afternoon crossing the Dee in anticipation of the pleasures that I know will soon be mine. Twenty minutes later I'm in one of those lovely little lanes that penetrate the Clwydian hills and lead the traveller westwards towards Denbigh and Ruthin. The hedgebanks are still full of late-flowering plants – bright yellow splashes of toadflax, the blue softness of scabious, and blowsy banks of rosebay. But the lateness of the season is evident too: arching branches of bright red rose-hips and great clumps of ink-black elderberry brush against the car as I drive by. Already the hills enfold me, and the softness of the landscape becomes part of me; for to enter this world is to take on some of its character, its spirit, into one's own spirit.

I leave the car, closing the door gently: to make even that noise seems a sacrilege in this place, where the only sound is of the breeze breathing through the pine branches, and the call of a sheep on a distant fellside. Every sense is stimulated in this spot, but in a very gentle, very delicate way: the light slanting through the trees is soft; the sounds of birds, of rustling in the brambles – even the far-away drone of a tractor haymaking on the meadows – are subdued, as if heard through a filter; and the scents – of earth, of moisture, of heather moors – are softly sweet, sensuous even.

The woods are soon left behind, and suddenly fastness becomes vastness; the enclosing woods and vale are lost below, and one is thrown into air, and light, and space. I recall the words of Richard Jefferies, the great naturalist who came to a similar place one day a hundred years ago in Wiltshire:

> Moving up the sweet short turf, at every step my heart seemed to obtain a wider horizon of feeling; with every inhalation of rich pure air, a deeper desire. The very light of the sun was whiter and more brilliant here. By the time I had reached the summit I had entirely forgotten the petty circumstances and the annoyances of existence. I felt myself, myself.

The air up here is warm, and sweet, sweetened by the scent of a million heather-flowers that sweep in a carpet of mauve from hilltop to hilltop, broken only by the narrow ribbons of pathways that etch a way along the undulating ridge.

The breeze, flowing from the west, is gentle and beautiful on this warm afternoon, having passed over a thousand Welsh hilltops, each adding something to its magical quality. I stand on a rocky outcrop, filling my lungs until they hurt with this honey-sweetness, absorbing its power until it flows into and beyond every pore in my body – cleansing, enriching, sweetening.

But this nectarine potion makes my body languid, and I nestle into a soft hollow in the ancient Celtic entrenchments, where the turf is soft and green. Here, close to the ground, the scents of the air are lost, pushed out by the scents of the earth – less sweet, but no less intoxicating. I lie back, in a position where, in one sweep of eyes, I can take in the hazy majesty of Snowdon's summit 30 miles distant, and the stalks of grass and bilberry-leaves just inches from my face.

I can think of no finer place in which to be on this beautiful September afternoon. My soul is content – nay, more than that – ecstatic – and at peace with itself and with the world. My soul prays a prayer of thanks to our Creator for such beauty and such peace . . . my eyes close in the mid-afternoon sunshine, and I drift into and out of dreams – dreams in which the spirits of those who lived on these heights in past millennia pervade my own spirit.

A shadow comes across my face, hides the sun. My body grows cold, and I awake to find the sun gone behind a great cloud-bank that has spilled in from the Irish Sea. The magic of the day is still here, but the day has changed. A threshold has been crossed, and I must move on. The wine has stood too long in its glass: the sparkle has gone. Yet my heart is as full of the pleasures of the day as was Jefferies' all those years ago:

> The silky grass sighs as the wind comes carrying the blue butterfly more rapidly than his wings. A large humble-bee burrs round the green down against which I rest; my hands are scented with thyme. The sweetness of the day, the fullness of the earth, the beauteous earth – how shall I say it?

# Alone in the Berwyns

*The joys and fears of solitude in the hills*

'NOT WITH THE BEST OF COMPANIONS would I hike over the Berwyns at night when the wind is high and the rain hisses from the tops of the rocky places . . .' So wrote Cledwyn Hughes over fifty years ago – words that came rushing back to taunt me one early-autumn day recently towards the end of a lovely walk over these little-known hills not far from Llangollen.

The morning had started with bright sunshine and blue skies. From my starting-point at Glyndyfrdwy – ancient dwelling-place of Owain Glyn Dwr, medieval 'Prince of All Wales' – the peaks of Llantysilio Mountain stood sharp against the sky, and the Dee cascaded noisily along the vale after several hours' overnight rain.

You cannot see the Berwyns from the Vale of Dee; you get no idea of their character from the lowlands. When asked to name Welsh peaks, most mention the Snowdon range, the Arans, the Rhinogs, the Arennigs, the Carneddau. Few think of the Berwyns, yet with Cadair Bronwen at almost 2,600 feet, these are indeed real mountains: not craggy, like most Welsh peaks, but huge, rounded masses of heather, bracken and grass, their lower slopes the home of sheep-farmers. Because of their relative obscurity, they are great heights for those who want a few hours where they will meet no living being except sheep and curlews, and hear no sound except that of the wind moaning through the heather.

I hiked up the Nant y Pandy, following the stream cascading down the gorge towards the Dee, the bright October sunlight golden on the changing woodland leaves. This is a place of mosses, ferns and lichens – draped across every rock and boulder, clothing the ruins of ancient mine-workings, and sprouting from every nook and crevasse along the nant.

Leaving the woods after a mile or so, the character of the Berwyns shows itself as the landscape opens out – first, grazing-pastures with wonderful, overgrown hedgerows of mountain-ash and elder; then bracken-covered slopes which give way to high-lands of heather interspersed with rush-clad bogs and small rivulets.

Man has ravished these mountains for rock and minerals, but his old, derelict workings are now part of the character of the place: disused tramways cut across the contours; pulley-shafts cut straight as a die up the mountainsides; levels cascade their rubble to the valley-floor; and roofless huts and shacks become ghost-places amongst the bracken.

It's a hard scramble to the tops, but well worth the effort: a 360-degree panorama of range after range – to the north, Llantysilio Mountain, with the familiar and much-loved Clwydians behind, leading the eye to the distant sea; westwards, the peaks and crags of Snowdon; southwestwards, Cadair Idris and the Rhinogs; to the south, the hills and moors around the Ceiriog and Tanat Valleys; and eastwards, the lesser heights towards Llangollen.

I could see my return route along the humpy ridge towards Vivod, but feeling weary, I found a soft hollow in the heather and, my ruck-sack for a pillow, dozed in the warm afternoon sun. Awakening an hour later, I felt a chill in the air that I'd not noticed previously. Springing to my feet, the sky to the north was still blue and clear; but in the opposite direction, the southern horizon was a continuous blanket of blackness, signalling a stormy weather-front moving rapidly towards the Berwyns.

Knowing I still had several miles hillwalking before dropping to safer ground, I put a spring in my stride and followed the track through the heather, the sky above darkening all the time. With the approaching storm ever menacing, I recalled the tales of the Hounds of Hell that are said to haunt these heights – blood-red hounds driven by the devil as their huntsman. At night-time and on dark stormy days these dogs drive the souls of the recently dead to their eternal fate, but will also drive to destruction those whom they encounter on the moors, the only protection being to create a crucifix of stones to keep the hounds at bay.

With the wind picking up and the sky darkening about me, the beauty of these hills was evaporating rapidly, and it was with great relief that I picked up the gravel-lane that led me down to the valley of the Dee, and back to civilisation. My time alone in the Berwyns had been wonderful, but it was good to be back among the life of the valley again. And later, sitting in the churchyard of the parish church of Glyndyfrdwy with the darkness of evening descending, I glanced up towards the storm-clouds gathering above the hill-tops, and knew in my heart and soul that Cledwyn Hughes was right . . .

(Cledwyn Hughes wrote several books about North Wales in the middle years of the last century, including *Poaching Down the Dee* and *A Wanderer in North Wales*)

# Will you still love me tomorrow?

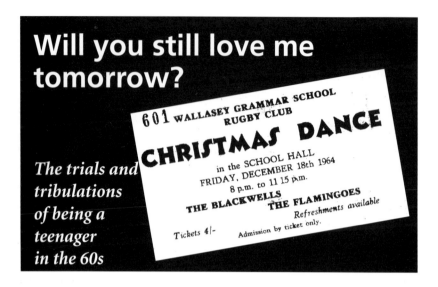

*The trials and tribulations of being a teenager in the 60s*

**601** WALLASEY GRAMMAR SCHOOL
RUGBY CLUB

**CHRISTMAS DANCE**

in the SCHOOL HALL
FRIDAY, DECEMBER 18th 1964
8 p.m. to 11 15 p.m.

THE BLACKWELLS   THE FLAMINGOES
*Refreshments available*

*Tickets 4/-*   Admission by ticket only.

IT FELL OUT of an old diary I had rediscovered as I was sorting through some boxes in the loft, and it started a flood of memories of a period in my life of challenge and change.

It was just a rather innocuous-looking piece of yellow-white card with the words

**Wallasey Grammar School**
CHRISTMAS DANCE

printed on the front. 'CHRISTMAS DANCE' was printed in one of those esoteric typefaces that were all the rage in the mid-sixties and which heralded the later pop-art movement in youth culture. Beneath were the two groups (yes, they were called groups in the sixties – bands in those days meant Joe Loss or Ted Heath): The Blackwells and The Flamingoes. The date? Friday 18th December 1964.

Suddenly, images of a dank, wet winter evening in the Wallasey of forty years ago came flooding back to life.

Excitement started about school lunchtime, when the talk would be about the forthcoming evening: Who were we going with? What are the groups like? Does anyone have a spare ticket? Afternoon lessons could be virtually written off, for teenage minds were on the activities of the coming evening hours rather than the aridity of Boyle's Law or second declension Latin verbs.

Then it was the race home, dinner, and a lengthy session in the bedroom deciding what to wear: the pink shirt or the check shirt? A collar-pin or not? Hipsters or cords? Then another hour in the bathroom for liberal applications of Brylcreem, Brilliantine and lashings of after-shave – or perhaps a peroxide rinse . . .

The Grammar dances were always held in the main school hall at Withens Lane: but what had been an austere school assembly hall at 9am was transformed by 8pm to a magical dance-hall of coloured lights and streamers. The stage, where only a few hours previously the Head and prefects had sat on time-hallowed oak chairs presenting the notices for the day, was stacked high with amps, speakers and microphones, with yards of black wire snaking across the platform. Into the hall streamed the youth of Wallasey, eagerly anticipating an evening of music, dance and . . . fun.

Only those who went to the dances know the gut-penetrating thrill as the lights went low and the first group went into action. Speakers vibrated, drums pounded – and for the first half-hour all stood and watched the lads on the stage. Gradually, though, the girls on the floor started to dance – in small groups at first, or in pairs. Then the more courageous boys joined in, usually singling out a particularly sought-after girl to dance with.

The mid-evening interval offered soft drinks and crisps at the back of the hall – but the older (and not-so-older) teenagers managed to sneak out of an unsecured window to the Saddle pub for a pint or two. And so the evening drifted on: the dancers becoming more relaxed, more confident; and relationships – boy–girl partnerships – formed amidst the heat, the noise, the sweat. Towards the end of the evening, couples danced closer, embracing, kissing. A casual visitor to the third-form cloakrooms would have heard sighings and rustlings from amongst the piles of navy macs and beige dufflecoats . . .

During the final number – usually 'Save the Last Dance for Me' or

'Will You Still Love Me Tomorrow?' – couples wandered off towards Liscard arm in arm, oblivious to the drizzly Wallasey night of Mersey mists. 'Can I walk you home?' often led to boys thus missing the last bus, and many has been the long, lonely walk home in the dark, early hours of Saturday morning, only the lingering scent of the girl and the ringing of the evening's music a reminder of the pleasures of the previous four or five hours.

Saturday afternoon: and an eager dialling of phone numbers shared the night before, in the hope that she remembers you, and that – best of all – she would like to see you again. And if not – well, there's still the rest of the school holidays to look forward to, for there were only three dances each year, each on the last day of term.

Thus were the beginnings of courtship in the sixties – and many a long-surviving romance was started on the waxy oak floor of the grammar-school dance hall at a Rugby-club dance.

I looked nostalgically at the time-faded dance ticket again, turned it over and, written in a 15-year-old schoolboy's writing, was a long-forgotten girl's name.

And a phone number.

*Will you still love me tomorrow?*

An enchant-
ing walk
home on the
longest night
of the year

# Midwinter's night

IT WAS THE LONGEST NIGHT of the year: the solstice of
winter. It had been a mild Sunday, typical of the pre-Christmas
period in these parts – a sweet, gentle breeze had blown in from the
south-west quadrant, bringing with it clouds and a drizzly dampness;
but quite pleasant, nonetheless.

I found myself in Wallasey during the afternoon, on family business: Christmas sherry and a warm room had instilled within me a
lethargy that I wished to shake off so, about 4pm, as dusk gathered
outside and the street lamps started to come on, I decided I would
shirk the car and walk home, to Thurstaston.

It was a walk I had done many times before, but always on fine
spring or summer afternoons, following the westering sun and enjoying the beauty of Wirral's coast, heaths and woods in their daylight
glory. This would be different: the paths, the places, the sights and the
sounds of daytime would wear a new complexion on this, the darkest
day of the year.

New Brighton's suburban streets were dusky, homely: Christmas-
trees and gaily-coloured flashing lights illuminated every living-room
window; but these were soon left behind, to be replaced by the wide,
deserted pavements of the promenade. There was little sign of the

imminent festive season here, only a billboard poster promoting the post-Christmas *Cinderella* pantomime at the Floral Pavilion. The old cliff-line above and beyond the Red Noses, grassy acres which in summer are bedecked with flowers and butterflies, looked dark and mysterious. Behind me, the lights of Liverpool glowed brightly; but ahead, where my way led, the street-lights petered out and the inky winter's night began. Away to the north, the smells and sounds of the sea were to be my companions for the next five miles or so; here crashing noisily against the vertical face of the promenade wall, but soon to give way to the quieter but still persistent wash on the gentle slope of the embankment.

With the comforts of the civilised world now left well behind, I was alone in the darkness of the evening; the narrow strip of white concrete ahead – my path atop the embankment – was clear, for the clouds reflected much light from inland Wirral. With a receding tide leaving the sands wide and wet, wading-birds – oyster-catchers and curlew – foraged noisily for food, their eery, ghost-like calls echoing across the wet flats. Way, way out to sea, lights twinkled – some from boats and ships out on Liverpool Bay; some from buoys and beacons warning of wrecks and banks, hazards of the deep.

Beyond Moreton, with its friendly lighthouse lit up and glowing on this dark winter's night, a long line of street-lamps in the distance gave promise of more promenade at Meols and Hoylake. But here, at Dove Point – one of the most deserted and lonely points on the north Wirral coast – I stopped to consider the folk of the past, our ancestors, who had eked out a meagre existence here. I gazed down at the silent sandbanks, glistening now in the light of a rising moon, to the remnants of the peat-beds of the submerged forest where men and women had lived in former times. They, more than we, would have been glad to see the passing of this night – the longest night – and to note the lengthening days towards spring, the warming of the land and sea, so vital to their very existence.

The long, lamp-lit promenade at Hoylake, with its cosy, warmly lit homes, seemed in sharp contrast to these thoughts of the past. The town's inns, busy tonight with folk enjoying a pre-Christmas drink, looked inviting; but I knew that, once ensconced in their warm rooms, I would find it difficult to continue.

At Red Rocks I ran down the slipway to the beach and stood, entranced. Here indeed was another world: the clouds had dispersed from the sky above; and to the west over Wales, where there was no town-light to impinge, was an inky black, speckled with stars. Far, far away, by Hilbre, the sound of the sea was but a constant, distant murmur. Southwards, up the estuary, lights twinkled on both sides of the river, those on the Welsh side reflected by the waters of the ebbing tide.

I headed across the sands and into the moonlight, around the Marine Lake, and into old West Kirby. The congregation of St Bridget's were singing carols on this Sunday night before Christmas, and the words and music stayed with me as I continued through Caldy, tired now but within hailing distance of home.

Beyond Caldy, I had to choose between the dark way across the hill and through the woods, or by the main road. The night was still fine, the moon was high and bright, so I entered the unknown world of Thurstaston at night. Here were ways which, in daytime were obvious, pleasant and clear; but on this, the longest night, even with a bright moon, were strange and mysterious. Trees and crags towered above my path, blocking out the moonlight; branches caught my hair; and my feet tripped on a thousand twisted roots. Yet I was unafraid. This was a place which I knew and loved. There was no fear here, no evil; this was a place where I and my children played amongst the heather on sunny June afternoons, where we picnicked and frolicked together in the warm sunlight.

On the summit ridge I stood on that longest night, looking down to where our parish church nestled in the bare-branched trees. In a few days, folk would be worshipping the new-born Christ within those old and hallowed red-stone walls, singing carols of praise to our

Saviour, the God who had created all the wonders I had experienced this evening. And within five minutes I would be home, with the family again, looking forward to sharing with them the joys of the Christmas season.

And by morning, the longest night of the year would be over.

(This first appeared in the *Wirral Journal*, Winter 1994)

# 'Dream often . . .'

*To my daughter, age 11,
on leaving Junior School*

I T'S A LOVELY JULY EVENING, and I'm walking over Thurstaston Hill behind your school. In a few moments I'll be collecting you from your Year 6 leavers' party – from high up on the heath I can hear music and youngsters' shouts coming up from the school hall. It sounds as though you're all having a great time – and so you should, for you are all celebrating a big milestone in your journey through life. It seems like only yesterday we let go of your tiny hand as you ran off to your classroom on your first day at school – your first important step into the big, big world outside the security of your home. Now you're on another threshold, and are about to leave the cosy life of this fine local school to enter the world of secondary education. It will be a huge step for you, and one which you'll embark on with excitement mixed with apprehension – and, dare I say it, a certain amount of fear.

But your little school has prepared you well for the future: its caring, professional, friendly teachers have played their part in forming not only your mind for future learning, but also your heart and soul for the even more important things in life – morality, honesty, integrity: concepts that the world at large seems to have forgotten in recent generations.

Yes, you've reached an important stage in your journey, for you are also on the verge of changing from a child into a woman – and that is even more scary than transferring from primary to secondary school. For as well as the physical changes that are transforming your body, you will be noticing the emotional upheavals that are, in one and the same day, or hour, driving you insane or making you feel on top of the world . . .

And so, my dear, what words of advice can a father give to his daughter: you who, in the school hall down below are one moment running around the place with excitement like a six-year-old; then minutes later are showing the sophistication of a young adult?

First, enjoy and savour every moment of your youth. Time, to you, seems eternal: but you'll soon be looking back on these days with a wistful eye. Do not become one who reminisces and says, 'I wish I'd done that when I was young': if you can, do it now, or soon – for the days, weeks and years soon pass, and there's nothing worse than living a life full of regrets. I have a small booklet depicting the history of your little school. On one of the pages is a faded photo of the pupils standing in the sunny playground for the photographer a hundred years ago. The girls and boys look eager and fresh-faced, as you do today. They too ran around the school shouting and shrieking, as you do this evening. But time has gone by: those youthful faces are no more. Those boys and girls have lived their teenage years, their years of youth, their middle years and their years of old age. All are gone. All that is left is a faded old photo. So enjoy every minute of every day: do not say 'I'll do it tomorrow' – do it today if you can!

Then strike a fair balance between work and play. Take time to enjoy the beautiful things in life – which are also usually the most important. Fill your mind and soul with those things that uplift the heart and spirit: good reading, good music, good friendships. Go only to those places which edify the person; shun bad company; keep out of temptation's way.

Keep firm your belief in the creator God who made you and the wonderful world around you. Enjoy, admire and conserve the beautiful things of his creation: the landscape and all its living things. Seek out the vastness of the cosmos; enquire within yourself and outside yourself about the meaning of life, and of the spiritual life of your heart and soul.

Use every moment of every day wisely: wake early, savour the freshness of dawn; listen to the wise voices of the past; learn from the experiences of others; eat wisely; dream often; take time out of the bustle of daily living to be with your Self: listen to your heart; look often at great works of art; listen to the world's greatest music; read the best literature ever written; enjoy the song of birds; look at the pattern on a butterfly's wings, or the sunlight and shadow on spring-time leaves; watch the sky for beautiful sunsets.

Keep close to your family and those friends who are dearest to you. Repay trust with integrity. Never go to sleep with anger in your heart: settle quarrels before they start. Give grateful thanks for others' kindly acts.

These are some of the things that we, and your teachers at your school have been quietly but carefully getting across to you, because they know they are the things that are worthwhile in life. Sadly, many grow up to forget about such things: they are the ones who drift aimlessly through life, never really knowing who they are, or where they are going. They grow up to be only half-human, their heads full of canned rubbish, unable to see beyond the shutters of their closed minds.

In a few minutes, I'll be leading you away from your leavers' party: your ears will be full of music, and your heart will be full of emotions. Treasure the moment.

And as you walk down School Lane with me, take a glance back-wards to your old school, with thankfulness for the past in your heart, and excitement about the future in your eyes . . .

# The white month

*My favourite time of the year*

UNHESITATINGLY, IT MUST BE THE TIME of the May-blossom: that brief but ever-so-beautiful spell towards the end of spring and on the brink of summer when our land responds to the warming weather and lengthening days by throwing a blanket of creamy-white blossom across the countryside.

But the anticipation of this beautiful week in May often starts way back in late January or early February when, in these mild western lands influenced by the Atlantic Gulf Stream, we may see the hawthorn buds swelling pink and, perhaps in one or two very sheltered spots, even showing a leaf or two of green. Then, in the cold drabness of those late-winter days, the mind is suddenly taken forward to the warmth and light of a May day, and we know then that, despite the cold still to come, winter's misery will indeed eventually give way to the delights of spring and summer.

But how often are we teased by the slowness of the coming of the May-blossom? Most years a few warm, sunny days in April bring forth the bud-clusters, and we tell ourselves that 'the May will soon be in flower'. Then the cold sets in again with the coming of the month itself, and the blossoming is put on hold again, perhaps for weeks. All around, the leaves are opening on oak and ash, despite the adverse weather: but the May-blossom buds remain tightly shut, awaiting the coming of warmer, sunnier days.

But come they do – typically in the second or third week in May – when an anticyclone will sit itself firmly over the British Isles for a week, and suddenly the skies are clear, the sun is out from dawn to dusk, and the temperature is up in the seventies. That is the week of the May-blossom. Up and down our land, hedgerows, already wearing the fresh green of spring, become adorned with a garland of cream. At the edges of copses and woods, branches become heavy with flowers. In the stillness of the hazy, mid-day heat, the air wears only one scent: that of the May-blossom. Buttercup-yellow meadows become transformed from yellow canvases to white-framed works of art.

What is there about this annual display of nature's profusion that pulls at the very heart-strings of our soul? Is it the sheer vastness of the display? Or the individual beauty of a single flower? Perhaps, for many of us, it's the connection of May-blossom with childhood and youth: fond and, perhaps, wistful memories of endless, sun-filled days when we played freely in the carefree world of our childhood. Or perhaps the May-tree has more romantic associations as we recall lying in its shade with our loved one on a warm spring evening.

Perhaps it's much deeper than that. For the blossoming of the May comes at a time when the whole of creation seems to be at its peak. The birdsong is at its richest, the foliage of the trees is at its most luxuriant, the grasses are lush and running to flower . . . the flowering of the May comes at the climax of the most exuberant few weeks that nature can muster.

Sadly – and like many a romance – the long-awaited moment of fulfilment and passion is soon gone: a few hot days in late May, or a drenching from a thundery cloudburst, and the beauty of the May-blossom is reduced to a few sad, rusty-coloured remnants hanging from trees and hedgerows. Or a day of strong westerlies will send cascades of 'summer snowflakes' fluttering to the ground, making white the path-edges of our countryside.

The passing of the May-blossom also signals the end of spring and the beginning of summer: and we know that the next display of the May-tree will be that of the scarlet berries of autumn.

However, even after the flowering of the May is over here, I can, if I wish, re-visit the experience: for, way up in the cooler regions of the Welsh hills, the May-trees flower later than in the milder, lowland areas in which I live. In late June, when the scent and sight of the May-flowers are but a distant memory, I can, in a short drive, regain the lost beauty that means so much to me, and relive, albeit briefly, my favourite week of the year.

# Thunderstorms over Thor's Stone

IT HAD BEEN ANOTHER LONG, swelteringly hot, sultry summer's day. We'd had no rain for weeks, and the earth was parched and cracking. The birches on the heath were shedding their leaves early, the branches on the great horse-chestnuts on the fringes of the wood were drooping, and even those low-lying swampy bogs between the sand-dunes and the beach had dried up, leaving only a fantastic mosaic of cracks and crevices in the baked ground.

The weathermen had forecast storms spreading north from the continent for days, but they had reached as far as Shropshire and then drifted east, bestowing their life-giving rain on counties other than ours – and so Cheshire continued to shrivel up, its heaths and pastures, its mosses, woods and shorelands parched to the core. Was there to be no end to this unnatural spell of weather – the sort which, so welcome at first, soon becomes monotonous in its predictability, pervading earth, sea and sky, and bleaching out that colourful dimension that makes the British landscape so very special?

The change when it came was subtle – an almost imperceptible shifting in the direction of the breeze, a slight change in the quality of light, and a vague smell in the air that heralds an advancing thunderstorm. It's something I have always loved – the anticipation, the excitement of an approaching storm. But would this one pass us by, like its recent predecessors . . . or would we get the drenching that we so badly needed?

4 pm: the first few clouds in days blow up from the south-east and hide the sun – a relief in itself after the scorching rays of recent weeks. But there's still more blue sky than grey . . .

7.30 pm: The sky is now 100 per cent leaden, and in the distance are the first vague rumbles of thunder. The birds have fallen silent, and a cold wind rustles the leaves in the garden trees. I put on my boots, search for my waterproof, and head out through the woods onto the heath – so arid that even the heathers are shrivelling up. On the top ridge I look down towards the meadows which sweep westwards towards the Dee – usually so green and verdant, they are varying shades of yellow, umber and ochre, enhanced by the strange quality of this pre-storm light.

The crack, when it comes, takes me by surprise: a bolt of light and sound from the leaden skies overhead that sends shivers of shock down my spine. I scurry from the exposed ridge, chased by the first spots of rain, eastwards towards the lower land around Thor's Stone. Thor: god of the thunder, god of the chariots, god of the gods. I stand against the rough redness of this rock of rocks and watch the rain cascading down its gulleys and chasms as thunder and lightning, light and sound, echo around the natural amphitheatre.

One almost hears the plants and trees that bedeck this mysterious place lapping up the life-giving water after weeks of drought. Even in the gathering dusk one can see their sagging forms become sharp again, erect, as the life-liquid is taken up by roots, leaves and branches.

And the scent in the air now is like no other: an almost sensual odour of rain and chlorophyll and earth and peat and leaves and bark and grass . . .

But the storm soon passes: the sky lightens towards the west and I scramble up to the summit-ridge again to survey a different earth: one that has tasted the sweet touch, not of the god of gods, but of the God of gods – One who has the power to wave a wand of goodness across a needy earth, to make fields and pastures green again, to revive dusty spirits and to renew life in magical and mysterious ways. And I am refreshed.

# The well at the World's End

## *A lifetime's search for an elusive Welsh spring*

I'VE BEEN SEARCHING FOR IT since I was a youngster; the classic fairy-tale 'The Well at the World's End' caught my imagination more than most, for my parents would often take us to that enchanted place called 'World's End' enfolded in the Eglwyseg hills near Llangollen. The story tells of a young girl whose stepmother told her to take a sieve and bring it home full of water from the well at the World's End. Not knowing either where the well was, nor how to fill a sieve with water, she was helped on her way by advice from various folk, including a frog who demanded from her whatever he wanted in return for his help.

That evening the frog turned up at the girl's home and made various requests, finally asking that she chop off his head. This she did, reluctantly, whereupon the frog changed into a handsome young prince who had been under the spell of a wicked magician. The actions of the girl had broken the spell and, needless to say, they married and lived happily ever after . . .

Thus began my quest for the well at the World's End.

My fascination throughout most of my life for tracing ancient springs and wells has taken me into some of the wildest and most far-flung corners of the British Isles; and rarely have I failed in my quest. Hours I have spent scrambling into fern-clad rocky ravines on the west coast of Anglesey, or into boggy hollows in Galloway, or on

Lleyn's remotest corners, or Ireland's wild Atlantic coast. Almost always I have been rewarded by the magic of discovering some long-lost saint's spring, or holy healing well, often with cool crystal-clear water bubbling up from the dark, peaty depths of the land.

Yet here is an old well virtually on my doorstep that has eluded me for nigh-on thirty years. Many times have I come to that cleft in the hills to search it out, and by many routes. Sometimes, walking from Llangollen town by the Dee or by the canal bank, past the ancient, hallowed stones of Valle Crucis and Eliseg's pillar. Sometimes, over craggy Dinas Bran and along the escarpment of the Eglwyseg rocks. Occasionally, across the heather-clad moors of calling curlew and eternal winds. And each time I have scrambled about the rocks and streams between Craig-y-Adar and Craig-y-Forwyn searching for a likely spring that fits the name and the story.

And I'm in good company, for others before me have made similar pilgrimages. William T. Palmer, the little-known yet superb writer of local landscapes, went in search of the well in the 1930s. In *The Verge of Wales* he says,

> The well at the World's End has romance and terror in its very name; its position should be shrouded in mystery, its waters sparkling and stark and pure. It should be difficult to approach, give strength to body and soul, and be dangerous to leave. A Pilgrim's Progress sort of place, with a touch of William Morris giving hectic contrast in colour and beauty, in form and outline – a cold and ethereal well.

Dixon Scott, the young Liverpool journalist whose life ended all too sadly on a hospital ship at Gallipoli in 1915 at the young age of 34, and who was described by Max Beerbohm as one who 'loved the very feel of language' wrote in *The Liverpool Courier* early in the last century of his pilgrimage to the World's End.

I came to a place where vast constellations of primroses, twinkling galaxies of primroses, ropes and dripping branches and golden swarms of primroses, flashed exultantly upon a vermeil firmament . . . and after that I came to the place of rocks; some of the rocks were livid, some were grey, and some, in the bed of the stream, were of the colour of ancient bloodstains. The voice of the stream echoed through all this place in a continuous and proud lament.

Scott spends some time at the stream-side, as I have done so many times, taking in the awesome silence and grandeur of this place of buzzards and crows and crags and firs. But in the end he leaves it strangely unsatisfied, unfulfilled: 'It was an unanswered enigma I told myself as I climbed up the rocky pathway that led to the upper world; it was an unfinished phase, a broken song, an arrow turned in mid-flight. It was a story without an ending, a portrait with the face left blank. It was life itself.' And as he gained the moor-clad heights and the light and the fresher air of the uplands, he philosophised, 'To speak solemnly of the World's End now, to think with any desire of it and its dim, strange wells, became an utter foolishness. For here, mother-naked among the sweet immortal elements, terrible and magnificent with promises and possibilities, there lay outstretched before me the Beginning.'

Dixon Scott had gone looking for the well at the World's End hoping to find there fulfilment of some kind; instead, he came away having found a new beginning. The magic of the fairy-tale, of the young girl finding a new beginning at the end of a quest, had spoken through the ages to a heart and spirit open to the wonders of the landscapes of life in all their richness and mystery.

And have *I* found the well at the World's End, or am I still searching? That would be telling!

# Timeless!

## *The magic of Choral Evensong*

I GO WHEN I FEEL THE CALL TO GO: I may be in my study, working on an ordinary weekday afternoon – and suddenly, out of the blue, I'm in my car and driving south along the High Road to my county city. It's a strong call when it comes, and I can never resist it. I just know I have to be there.

I park the car, and am soon among the remnants of shoppers and city workers making their way home. Of all the thousands of folk whom I pass on the way, it's strange to think that probably none are going to where I'm going: their minds are on the evening meal, or their plans for the evening.

I'm on a timeless quest, following in the footsteps of countless others who have responded to this call down the centuries. I weave my way along the city's narrow, twisting cobbled streets, past half-timbered buildings, or along the ancient Rows, to the heart of Chester. The buskers are packing up their flutes, guitars and hats-full of coins; shop-assistants are pulling down the shutters; it's day's-end for them – but for me, the day holds another dimension.

The magic starts with first glimpse of the cathedral: in the sharp, cold sunlight of spring; the dappled warmth of summer; the mellow softness of autumn; or the floodlit glow of winter. Whatever the season, whatever the weather, whatever my mood, first sight of the cathedral lifts my spirits. If I'm early, and it's a fine spring or summer's evening, I'll go and sit among the bluebells under the trees on the grass behind the cathedral and watch the folk walking along the city walls.

Then, about ten minutes before Evensong, I'll go inside. Here, on hot summer days, the coolness is a welcome relief after the hot dusty city streets. On cold winter nights the welcoming warmth cheers the body as well as the heart. But whatever the time of year, the spirit of the cathedral wraps around one in a friendly way immediately on entering. Through the time-worn cloisters with their ancient grave-slabs, carved stones and decorated windows – all with a tale to tell of someone from its long, long history. Into the nave, where on a bright sunny evening the great west window throws cascades of colour into the huge spaces.

Past the magnificent wall-mosaics and little groups of visitors admiring the richness that this testimonial to mankind's faith over a thousand years displays in every nook and cranny, every stone and window, every buttress, column and roof-arch.

And into the dark privacy of the choir. Suddenly the vastness and majesty of the cathedral recede and the closeted confines of the stalls help the darting mind, still full of the images of city life, to pull in to the closeness of worship, to focus on the ritual about to be played out in this hallowed space.

Ten minutes in the richly carved choirstalls with their depictions of daily life and routine throughout the ages, and already the outside world is a thing apart, and the spirit of daily sung worship in this wonderful place enters the very depths of soul. The sounds of the city are gone; replaced by the sound of silence – worshipful silence, expectant silence, Godlike silence.

From somewhere seemingly far away, a shuffle on the stone floor signals the entrance of the choir as the notes of the organ rise to meet their arrival. They enter, take their seats, and Choral Evensong has started, following a ritual that has scarcely changed in five centuries of worship. Here, and simultaneously in dozens of other cathedrals across our land, faithful choristers and worshippers are taking time out at a particularly busy part of the day to offer up something that is indefinable. Through the music of psalms and anthems one is giving thanks to God for all that the day has brought our way, while at the same time offering petition for the coming night. One is also taking the thread of continuity across the aeons of time, reaffirming the faithfulness of countless worshippers across the ages who, like us, have committed themselves to offering up thanks, praise and petition in music.

The choir sings the anthem, and a particularly spine-tingling setting it is too. The words and music pull at the heart-strings; and as the final notes echo around the vast spaces of the cathedral, visitors pause and wonder – they too have got caught up in the mystery of worship in this great building.

The service is soon over, and as the choir process out of the stalls, they leave a sense of warmth, of fulfilment, behind as they go. The handful of worshippers gather up their possessions: some have dropped in while shopping, some are on their way home from work, some are visitors, some are regulars. We smile, say hello, and we are on our way. Outside, on sunny summer evenings the brightness of the daylight takes us by surprise; in wintertime we scurry through the wet, cold city streets, keenly anticipating a hot meal. The shopfronts are shuttered, all is quiet. In the 45 minutes within the cathedral, the city has gone to sleep.

But at any and every time of the year, one scurries home with a sense of completeness, of fulfilment of heart. A very special time in a very special place. Fabulous.

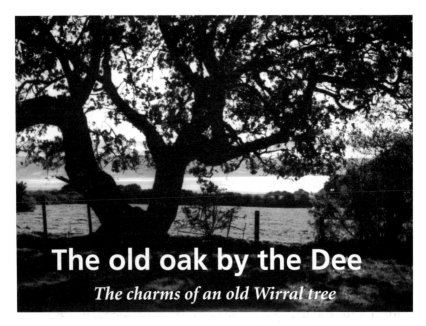

# The old oak by the Dee

## The charms of an old Wirral tree

I<small>T'S ONE OF MY FAVOURITE TREES</small>. There's nothing particularly spectacular about it though: it's not a majestic specimen standing proud in some fine Cheshire parkland. It's just a typical hedgerow oak at the edge of a small meadow at Oldfield, above the banks of Dee, near Heswall.

So what makes this so special for me?

Perhaps it is its shape. This is no straight, upstanding oak. At some time in its youth, its leading shoot was damaged – perhaps torn off by one of the many gales that sweep across the estuary onto Wirral lands, or eaten by an animal – and consequently it has thrown up two huge convoluted trunks skywards. And these form an almost perfect symmetry: gemini-like twin trunks that boldly spread an immense canopy across the tiny meadow which it borders. Yet at the same time the trunks look precarious – so finely balanced that it seems that it would take only a small force to bring the twin trunks crashing to earth.

Perhaps it is its age. By English oak standards, this is a positive youngster, but still a couple of hundred years old. This was a sapling when Victoria came to the throne. It would possibly have seen the ships of the Dublin Packet sailing along the Dee in and out of Parkgate. It would have watched the surveyors planning the route of the railway from West Kirby to Hooton just a meadow's-distance westwards. It would have heard the first peal of bells from the new parish church of St Bartholomew northwards towards Thurstaston. Throughout its long life it will have observed the coming and going of daily agricultural life on and around the fertile pastures that border these western banks of the Wirral Peninsula. It will have seen generations of farm-workers and agricultural workers and their families come and go, watching the yearly rituals of hay-making, hedge-trimming and the tending of cattle and sheep over the Oldfield acres. It will have seen too family outings of blackberry-pickers filling their containers from the ripe hedgerows that line these lovely Deeside pastures. Maybe it's these things that make this tree special to me.

Perhaps it is its position. I usually see this old oak as I walk down from the Dungeon in late afternoon, at a time of day when the sun is westering over the Welsh hills and shining up the waters of the Dee or sparkling off its wet sands and mudflats. Against this backdrop of incandescent light the old tree forms a perfect silhouette, the backlight showing up the fine detail of trunk, leaves and branches.

Perhaps too it is my imagination, for it's set in a part of Wirral that is full of magic and mystery. Close by is the Dungeon, that wild glen with its cave, and waterfall cascading over a rocky precipice. Higher up towards the ridge lies ancient Piper's Well, while old field names such as Grimes Croft speak of mystery and romance. Somewhere below my old tree, on the meadows below that border the river, lies the lost village of Warmby, tantalisingly refusing to reveal its secrets.

But of course the beauty of my old oak is a combination of all these things, and more; it's knowing that it shelters a rich variety of birds, mammals and insects; that it has provided shelter from winter storms, and shade from midsummer sun for generations of farm folk; that it is a living, enduring thing of beauty in all seasons – in spring, as the leaf-buds are bursting into new life and clumps of bluebells nestle at its roots; in summer, as it casts its shade over the adjoining pastures and hedgerows; in its golden autumn raiment of bronzing leaves that enrich the surrounding meadowlands as they fall into the soil; and in winter, when its true shape stands stark against the setting sun in mid afternoon.

My regular walk down to the Dee would be less rich without seeing my friend, the old oak; and it's a sobering thought that long after I'm gone from this life and this world, the tree will still be catching the late afternoon sunlight from across the sands of Dee, to delight the eyes and hearts of others with its many moods and facets.